F MARYLAND

in the Library of Congress

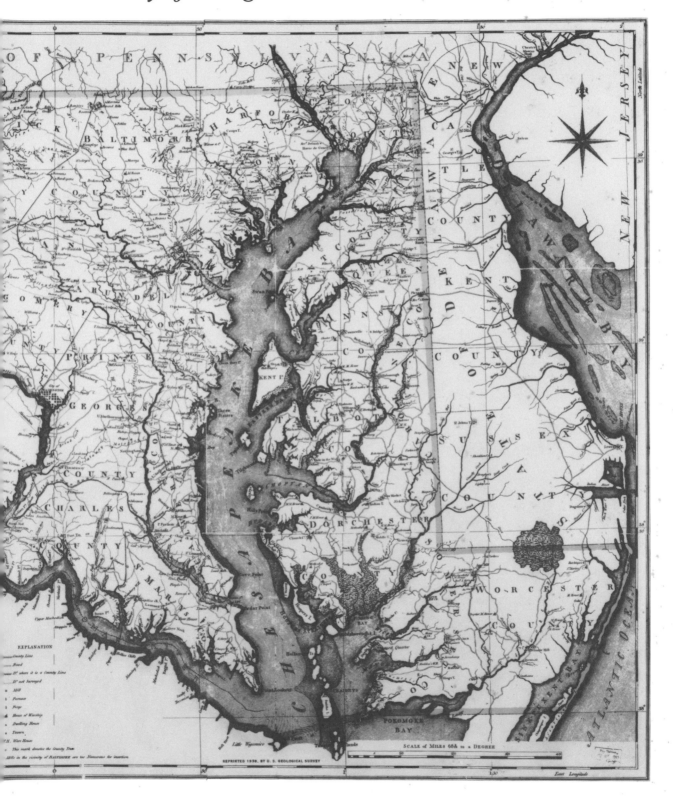

FROM A LIGHTHOUSE WINDOW

Recipes and Recollections
from the
Chesapeake Bay
Maritime Museum
St. Michaels, Maryland

All proceeds from the sale of this book are used to support the continuing projects, programs, and operations of the Chesapeake Bay Maritime Museum in accordance with its stated purpose of preserving the heritage of the Chesapeake Bay.

For additional copies, use the order blanks in the back of the book, or write directly to:

FROM A LIGHTHOUSE WINDOW
Mill St., P.O. Box 636
St. Michaels, Maryland 21663-0636
(410) 745-2916

Inquiries from organizations wishing to purchase the book for fund-raising purposes are invited.

First Printing: 10,000 September 1989
Second Printing: 10,000 September 1991
Third Printing: 10,000 February 1996

Library of Congress Cataloging-in-Publication Data:

Chesapeake Bay Maritime Museum.
    From a lighthouse window : recipes and recollections from the Chesapeake Bay Maritime Museum.
        p.   cm.
    Includes index.
    ISBN 0-922249-01-6
    1. Cookery—Chesapeake Bay Region (Md. and Va.) 2. Chesapeake Bay Region (Md. and Va.)—History.   3. Chesapeake Bay Region (Md. and Va.)—Social life and customs.   I. Title
    TX715.C5243   1989
    641.59755′18—dc20   89-9712
                                                              CIP

ISBN   0-922249-01-6

Printed in the United States of America by
Cadmus Journals Services, Easton, Maryland

The Chesapeake Bay Maritime Museum is dedicated to furthering interest, understanding, and appreciation of the culture and maritime heritage of the Chesapeake Bay and its tributaries through continuing educational activities including collection, documentation, exhibition, research, and publication.

Chairman
Linda Davis

Book Design
Julienne McNeer Burns

Cover Design
Beth Singer, Beth Singer Design
Washington, D.C.

Cover and Color Photography
Richard A. K. Dorbin, Paragon Light Studios
Annapolis and Easton, Maryland

Pen and Ink Illustrations
MaryAnn McNamara-Ringewald
Picture Editor
Ellen Plummer

Copy Editor
Barrie Dettling

Contributing Authors

Beverly Abribat	**James B. Foster**	**Haskell Tubiash**
John W. Cane	**Gloria Frost**	**George K. Tucker**
Linda Davis	**Jim Holt**	**Winnie Vaules**
Richard J. Dodds	**Ellicott McConnell**	**George Wagner**
	Ellen Plummer	
	MaryAnn Schwanda	

THE COOKBOOK COMMITTEE
Recipe Content Chairman, **Nancy Fletcher**

Galley Slaves:

Mary Ann Bradley	**Ginny Graebert**	**Rose Mary Mazza**
Marge Burke	**Gaby Haab**	**Ida Olcese**
Mary Doeller	**Hertha Holland**	**Edna Shaw**
Betsy Fisk	**Mary Louise Humiston**	**Ann Simmons**
Leslie Gleichman	**Lynn Jefferys**	**Ruth Weller**
	Betty Liskey	
	Sheila Mann	

Crew Members:

Eleanor Baker	**George Fisk**	**Ginger Munsell**
Joan Cole	**Bernard Girod**	**Lise Valliant**
Marge Eby	**Bé Holt**	**Helen Van Fleet**
Betty Egger	**Carol Kabler**	**Ruth Volin**
	Ellicott McConnell	

The Cookbook Committee would like to express grateful appreciation to the many donors of heirloom and special recipes from their private collections—We regret that we were unable to include all recipes submitted.

To those who lent photographs, postcards, and other memorabilia from personal family archives we are deeply indebted. It is our sincere hope that in preserving these treasures on the pages of **From a Lighthouse Window** *the memories they evoke will remain forever alive for you and your heirs.*

THE COOKBOOK COMMITTEE

ACKNOWLEDGMENTS

With Special Thanks to

Chesapeake Bay Maritime Museum
John R. Valliant, Executive Director and **Staff Members,**
Board of Governors, and **Volunteer Association,**
for support of and assistance to the book and the Cookbook Committee

and to

Beverly Abribat, for technical guidance;

Mark Adams, for his original recipe, "Rum Rosie," the grog that launched a cookbook;

The late **John Bowden,** of John Bowden Studio, Washington, D.C., for the enthusiasm and commitment he brought to this endeavor;

Archangel Antiques, Mary Ann Bradley—Proprietress, for the loan of antiques for cover photograph—redware bowl, granite ware saucer, two utensils, and basket;

David B. Baker, Jr., President, Board of Governors, Chesapeake Bay Maritime Museum, and President, Reese Press, Baltimore, for guidance and for making Reese Press experts available for consultation;

Big Al's Seafood Inc., for donation of seafood for cover photography;

Gilbert Byron, for introducing *From A Lighthouse Window*;

Mary Carolyn and **Sarah Cockey** on Maple Hall;

Richard J. Dodds, Curator, for tireless service to Cookbook Committee members and assistance in finding photographs and artifacts from the Museum's vast collection;

John Earle, Talbot County Historical Society and the Maryland Room, Talbot County Free Library, for general research assistance;

Mary Jane Fairbank and **Alice Haddaway** on The Jefferson Islands Club, Inc., and for historic recipes included in this collection;

Captain Ed Farley of the skipjack, *Stanley Norman*, and former crew member, **Mark Lichtenberger** on oystering and galley cookery;

Bill Harper on The Pasadena;

Bé and **Jim Holt,** for sharing their considerable knowledge;

Sonny Jackson, for donation of muskrats for recipe testing;

Mildred Kemp on Wades Point Farm;

Arthur H. Kudner, Jr., President, Tidewater Publishing Corporation and member of the Board of Governors, Chesapeake Bay Maritime Museum, for guidance and assistance;

Jim Lally, of the Museum's Photo Lab, for providing many photo prints;

Jack Larrimore, for permission to photograph Chesapeake Bay Retrievers Jukes and Jenna;

Little, Brown & Company, for permission to reprint from *Ogden Nash Verses*;

Mike Luby, Talbot County Historical Society, for assistance with historic photographs and recipes;

James A. Michener and **Random House, Inc.,** for permission to use quotations from *Chesapeake*, copyright 1978;

Scotty Oliver, Maryland Room, Talbot County Free Library, for general research assistance;

St. Mary's Square Museum, for permission to reprint the map of the Battle of St. Michaels from the booklet, "St. Michaels—The Town That Fooled the British";

Fritz Sonnenschmidt, Culinary Institute of America, Hyde Park, New York, and **Mary Ann Bradley,** for recipe conversions to low- or no-cholesterol alternatives;

Deenie Tyler, on skipjack galley cookery;

Jane Ward on Hooper Strait Lighthouse;

Waverly Press, for generous donations of time, talent, equipment, and technical expertise by many individuals at both the Baltimore and Easton locations;

C. Keith Whitelock, for permission to reproduce line drawings of Chesapeake Bay work boats, "Hull Profiles and Sail Plans;" and

Valerie Layman Youngs, for instruction in Eastern Shore cooking.

FOREWORD

The many facets of the view *From A Lighthouse Window: Recipes and Recollections from the Chesapeake Bay Maritime Museum*, reflect both the cultural and culinary heritage of the St. Michaels-Bay Hundred region of Maryland's Eastern Shore, as well as glimpses from around the Chesapeake Bay.

More than a simple cookbook, *From A Lighthouse Window* traces the lives and customs of the past along with the food and drink of those times. Historical anecdotes and relevant contemporary sketches, coupled with a collection of recipes gathered from family archives, old records, and interviews with countless local cooks reveal a picture of life on the Shore from a very special perspective.

The area's history described in these pages has also been preserved in part at the Chesapeake Bay Maritime Museum, through its exhibits, classes, and community activities. A major Museum project, this book represents the culmination of months of volunteer effort in outstanding gifts of time and talent.

On behalf of the Museum's Board of Governors and myself, we sincerely thank the numerous volunteers who participated in this project, and in particular we extend special thanks and congratulations to Linda Davis, project coordinator. Without her enthusiasm and dedication, this book might never have become a reality.

Just as the Museum's purpose is to present and preserve the Bay's history, so, too, *From A Lighthouse Window* seeks to illuminate such a journey back in time. It is hoped that through enjoyment of this book a new window will open on our understanding and appreciation of the rich legacy of the Chesapeake Bay.

John R. Valliant,
Executive Director
Chesapeake Bay Maritime Museum

INTRODUCTION

By Gilbert Byron

Before the coming of the automobile and the building of the bridge which now spans Chesapeake Bay, the island-like remoteness of the Eastern Shore produced a more leisurely way of living. It was before radios and television took more and more of our time, before frozen foods, and before microwave ovens replaced the heavy iron skillet.

In this earlier era, when every neck and finger of land in the Bay Hundred district of Talbot County had its own boatbuilder who left his individual mark on all of his craft, every locale also had its own talented cooks with their special recipes for teasing the taste buds of their families and friends (many of the best cooks were Black). These recipes—some recorded here for the first time—were passed down over many generations from mother to daughter, often by word-of-mouth. Some may have been brought from the Old World to America on sailing ships; others came from the colonists' encounters with new foods, and some may have come from the American Indians.

This was also an era when the bounties of the Bay Country were more plentiful than they are today. The Baltimore journalist, H. L. Mencken, once described the Chesapeake Bay Country as "a vast protein factory." Seafood—fish, oysters, clams, turtles, and the famous diamond-back terrapin—was high on this list, with wild waterfowl, Canada geese, and the canvasback duck close behind.

In this other era, every neck of land had its own summer boarding house that offered a temporary escape for harried city dwellers who were already experiencing Henry Thoreau's "quiet desperation." Wades Point Farm and Maple Hall, both near Claiborne, were active during this period, but almost any waterfront farm might take in a few paying guests during the summer. Each had its own special dishes, and some of these recipes were secretly guarded over the years.

Many of the large sailing craft, such as skipjacks and bugeyes, made Tilghman Island their home port during the oyster dredging season. All these sailing craft had cooks who were talented in serving foods that would satisfy these hardworking men who sailed the Bay during the winter. One old captain who sailed five different skipjacks during his career on the Chesapeake once told me of the huge trenchermen breakfasts he served his crews as they sailed for the oyster bars. Included were freshly baked biscuits, ham and eggs, fried potatoes, and even codfish cakes.

The editors of this cookbook have searched the Bay Country to find and record these special tested recipes that for generations have delighted the palates of easygoing Eastern Shore folks.

TABLE OF CONTENTS

A Sail Around· St. Michaels and Bay Hundred

St. Michaels and Bay Hundred were two of the political subdivisions of Talbot County, Maryland during the Revolutionary War. The term "hundred" derives from Old English, and originally designated either an area with 100 families or one which could supply 100 fighting men. Now it has survived to indicate a political section.

Talbot County's more than 600-mile shoreline is said to be the longest county shoreline in the U.S. According to the U.S. Geological Survey; the area includes 15 identified coves, 23 creeks, 7 necks or peninsulas, 5 harbors, and 7 islands. Add to this scores of locally-named and unidentified places and the true picture of this sprawling water-bounded territory begins to emerge.

Set sail at Oak Creek (1) near the community of Royal Oak. Originally called Bartletts Oak, it became known as Royal Oak possibly because two cannonballs were hung from one of the tree limbs as souvenirs of the British attack on St. Michaels in 1813. Nearby Newcomb, a stop on the Baltimore, Chesapeake and Atlantic Railroad from the ferry terminal at Claiborne, aided in Royal Oak's popularity as a vacation resort. Its celebration as "the healthiest place in America" was the result of a hoax perpetrated by a reporter on the *St. Michaels Comet* in 1874.

Passing the hamlet of Newcomb to port, sail under the Oak Creek Bridge and out into the broad Miles River. Dead ahead can be seen Miles River Neck (2) where several estates once owned by colonial and revolutionary aristocrats are still maintained today.

Turn to port and set course northwest to make the short haul to St. Michaels (3), originally named Shipping Creek. The name St. Michaels first appears in 1680, adopting the name from St. Michaels parish church; the St. Michaels River eventually evolved into the Miles River.

Next arrive at Parrott Point, location of the main defense during the British attack of 1813. On Fogg's Cove is the home of Samuel Hambleton, first purser of a naval squadron and designer of the "Don't Give Up The Ship" flag. To the north was the family home of the Hambletons, "Martingham" (4), patented in 1659.

ROSIE PARKS

The oyster dredging skipjack, Maryland's State Boat, was developed in the late 1800s. A premier example of the type is Rosie Parks, *one of the Chesapeake Bay Maritime Museum's floating exhibits.*

Built in 1955 by Bronza Parks of Wingate, Maryland, Rosie *measures 50 feet length on deck, has a 17-½ foot beam, and a draft of 3 feet with centerboard up. Though she worked the oyster bars for many years under Bronza Parks' brother, Captain Orville Parks, the "Admiral of the Chesapeake,"* Rosie *is one of the fastest skipjacks ever built. Under Captain Parks' command, she became one of the Bay's best-known skipjacks, winning most of the races she entered. Today,* Rosie *continues to maintain an enviable racing record.*

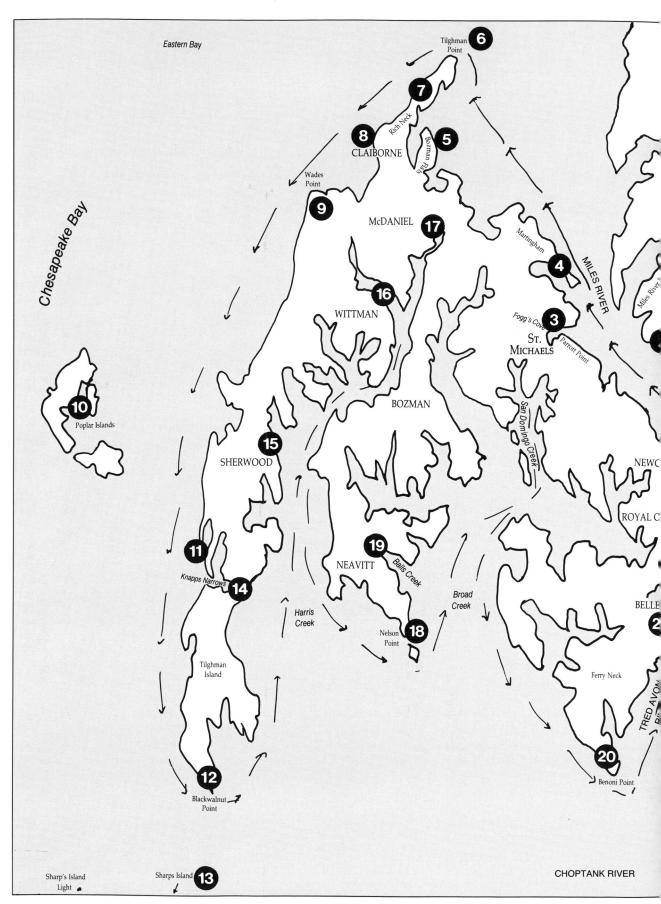

Eastern Bay

Tilghman Point **6**

7

Rich Neck

8
CLAIBORNE

Bozman Flats

5

Wades Point

9

McDANIEL

17

Martingham

4

MILES RIVER

Miles River

Chesapeake Bay

16

WITTMAN

Fogg's Cove

3

 St.
MICHAELS

Parrott Point

San Domingo Creek

BOZMAN

10

Poplar Islands

NEWC

15

SHERWOOD

ROYAL C

11

19

Balls Creek

NEAVITT

Broad
Creek

BELLE

Knapps Narrows

14

Harris
Creek

Nelson
Point

18

2

Ferry Neck

Tilghman
Island

TRED AVON

20

Benoni Point

12

Blackwalnut
Point

Sharp's Island
Light

Sharps Island **13**

CHOPTANK RIVER

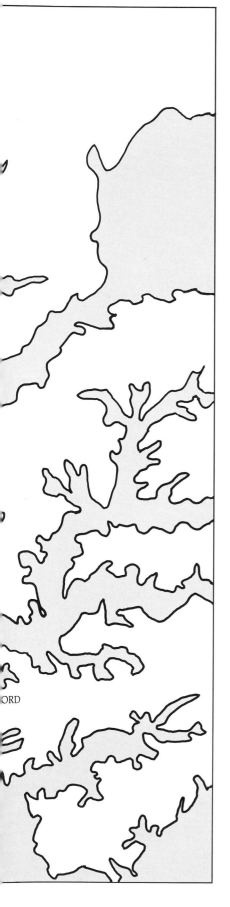

ORD

At Bozman Flats (5) a line drawn across to the northeast branch of Harris Creek would mark the boundary between the St. Michaels and Bay Hundred districts. The Miles River and Eastern Bay meet off Tilghman Point (6) on Rich Neck. The area from here to Blackwalnut Point on Tilghman Island has been called Bayside from earliest times. The road out of St. Michaels (now Route 33) was once named Bayside Avenue.

Rich Neck (7), assigned to William Mitchell in 1649, was the first tract to be claimed in Talbot County. By 1700 all of Rich Neck and most of Bayside was owned by the Tilghman family, the most notable being Matthew, who has been referred to as the "Patriarch of Maryland" and the "Father of Maryland Statehood." At the foot of Rich Neck is Claiborne (8), named for William Claiborne, the early Maryland settler.

Sailing southwest by Wades Point (9) and looking west to starboard, the remains of the Poplar Islands (10) can be seen. Only three small islands exist today of the 1,000-acre single island Claiborne named "Popeley" in 1631, after one of his lieutenants.

The first Talbot County land to be settled and farmed, it was also the site of a black cat farm established there in 1847 to supply pelts to Chinese furriers, but in 1848 the Bay froze over and the cats escaped to the mainland. During the 20th century an exclusive hunting and fishing club for affluent Democrats, The Jefferson Islands Club, Inc., functioned there as a retreat for presidents and legislators.

Knapps Narrows (11) marks the north end of Tilghman Island, which describes itself as a "home of the skipjacks." Named for Matthew Tilghman, one of its major owners, it was also known as Choptank Island on an 1877 map of the area.

Next, sail around Blackwalnut Point (12) into the Choptank River. Offshore to the south is Sharp's Island Light (13), all that is left of the 700-acre island that John Smith saw in 1608.

Pass the east end of Knapps Narrows (14) and enter Harris Creek. The communities of Sherwood (15), Wittman (16), and McDaniel (17) will be to port sailing north. Come about and sail out again with Bozman to port. Round Nelson Point (18) into Broad Creek; Neavitt (19) on Balls Creek will be to the west; then sail up San Domingo Creek to the west side of St. Michaels.

Come about again and head south around Benoni Point (20), sailing up the Tred Avon River with Oxford (21) to starboard and Bellevue (22) to port. The picturesque town of Oxford was the first capital of Maryland and, historically, a major port on the Chesapeake Bay. Established in 1683, the Oxford-Bellevue ferry is the oldest continually operating ferry on the Bay. Bellevue has existed as long as Oxford and is its western terminal. Originally called Ferry Neck, the community was later renamed by Oswald Tilghman for his wife, Belle. The cruise ends at Plaindealing Creek (23) just south of Royal Oak, less than one-half mile from its starting point.

13

·ST. MICHAELS BEGINNINGS
The 1700s

Early St. Michaels

Athe Oak Creek in New-comb, in about 1700, the surrounding countryside had been occupied by English-speaking settlers for one or two generations. Neither St. Michaels nor Easton existed yet as towns, although both the St. Michaels Church (1670s) and Talbot County Courthouse (1712) would eventually begin to gather settlements around them.

Oak Creek was at that time called "Harbor Rouse" after Robert Newcomb's plantation (1659) to the east, and it had many other names before becoming Oak Creek in the 19th century. The plantations to the west were James

Benson's "Benson's Choice" (1689) and "Benson's Enlargement" (1695). Several generations later they would be home to Perry Benson, hero of the Revolution and War of 1812. About a mile to the south stood "The Oak," later Royal Oak, a magnificent tree 40 feet in circumference, and the focal point of surveyor and ceremony.

St. Michaels, a significant center of commerce since the 18th century, is about three miles down the Miles River. The town occupies a narrow isthmus between the Choptank River and the Miles, an ideal location for St. Michaels Church, which could be reached easily by boat. As the colony grew, the location fostered commerce between the two river systems, and its peacefulness, simplicity, and charm have long made it a vacation and excursion spot.

When Captain John Smith explored the Chesapeake in 1608, a dense, primeval forest of oak, gum, maple, hickory, and pine covered the land. These are essentially the same species of trees, but with much larger specimens, that grow in the region today.

The land rush for the Miles River shore commenced in the 1660s. Old records from this era list surnames that are found in the local telephone book today.

The early 1700s were the golden years of the sotweed (tobacco) and the aristocrat. Oxford was the only town in Talbot County except for a few now-forgotten ports like Dover on the Choptank, remembered only by Easton's Dover Road. By the 18th century, it was possible to make your fortune in tobacco, but not by growing it. Planters took the risks and merchant traders reaped the profits.

The settlers were a rough and ready bunch, fighting, drinking, and carousing whenever they had a chance; the earlier period of puritanical moral codes was declining. Almost all travel and trade was by water except in severe weather and then only on foot or horseback until the mid-1700s.

John Hollingsworth received a land patent in 1664 and called it "The Beach," for its fine deep-water harbor, Shipping Creek, later called St. Michaels. From him it passed to Edward Elliot who, in 1677, acquired it for 8,000 pounds of tobacco. Elliot, a Scottish carpenter who later became a Maryland planter, built the first church on its present site. Shortly after 1900, men working in the street just a few feet from the church building dug up a wharf timber dating from the early days. The waterway used by the churchgoers was "Church Cove," narrow but deep enough for large boats until, over the years, townsfolk filled it in with rubbish. It is now occupied by Muskrat Park and the firehouse. The earliest legal record of the town (1680) mentions a horse race, indicating that people from nearby plantations gathered at this location for their social activities.

By the early 1700s the original log church had been replaced by a building constructed from lumber, and the land around it had been settled as farmland. Later in the 1700s the combination of deep water, timber, and expanding population made the area a natural spot for shipbuilding, and the town grew to accommodate the marine tradesmen that shipbuilding required.

BASTING SAUCE FOR BARBECUED CHICKEN
à la St. Michaels

The abundance of chicken farms on the Delmarva Peninsula has naturally resulted in the popularity of fund-raising barbecues for various organizations. This recipe has helped perpetuate the success of such functions and has been used by many area churches, the St. Michaels Volunteer Fire Department, and the local Miles River Yacht Club.

The recipe is recorded here for its future historical significance. At the height of its popularity during the '50s, '60s, and '70s, it is now somewhat untimely due to the current emphasis on reduced diet salt and general health consciousness.

PROPORTIONS FOR 100 CHICKEN HALVES
1 cup poultry seasoning
3 cups salt
5 teaspoons pepper
4 quarts cider vinegar
10 eggs, well beaten
2 quarts cooking oil

PROPORTIONS FOR A GRILL FULL
1-1/2 teaspoons poultry seasoning
5 teaspoons salt
1/4 teaspoon pepper
1 cup cider vinegar
1 egg, well beaten
1/2 cup cooking oil

In a large garbage can mix dry ingredients together; add vinegar and eggs, combining thoroughly. Blend in cooking oil thoroughly (with a clean mop handle; stir as often as necessary to re-blend).

Baste chicken halves with a previously unused johnny mop and don fireman's orange fluorescent gloves to turn chicken frequently. Grill 50 to 60 minutes.

THE BATTLE OF ST. MICHAELS

"On a dark and stormy night" in August 1813, the people of St. Michaels awaited an invasion by the large British fleet headquartered on Kent Island. As a shipbuilding center and port, the town was a prime target. For months the London newspapers had been demanding that the Admiralty search out and destroy such nests of raiders that were running the British blockade.

St. Michaels, a town of 60 houses and 300 people, had been preparing since spring for the attack. A 500-man county militia was quartered in the town's churches and camped in St. Mary's Square. Under the command of General Perry Benson, local Revolutionary War hero, the defenders had constructed a log boom across the harbor, with a fort on Parrott's Point at the south end. It was Benson who ordered lanterns hung in the trees to confuse British observers downriver. Refugee workers and their families crowded into the Onion Hill area from the shipyards on San Domingo Creek, while 40 St. Michaels men manned the two guns in the fort, peering over the earthworks and looking for the enemy.

Admiral Warren on his flagship *San Domingo* in Eastern Bay ordered the attack to be led by Lieutenant James Puckinghorne with an invasion force of 300 marines and sailors. At about 4 a.m. on August 10th, Puckinghorne's 11 barges reached their destination upriver from the

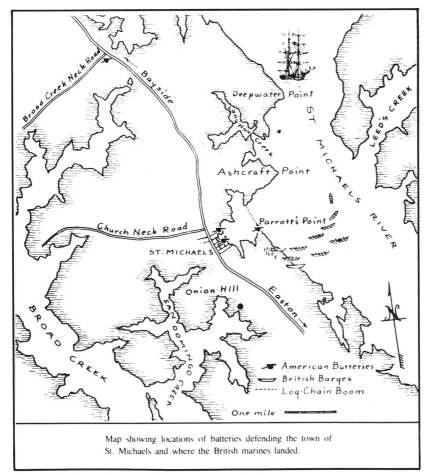

Map showing locations of batteries defending the town of St. Michaels and where the British marines landed.

16

fort. The brig *Conflict* had towed them past the town on the opposite shore of the Miles River. Groping through the rain and mist, the British surprised the fort's small force of defenders in the dark. There was only time to fire the two guns and run or swim to the town, where all defenders arrived safely. Accounts of the battle vary, but the British claim the destruction of the fort and a successful reembarkation, although Admiral Warren's original order had directed only a "search of armed vessels supposed to be in St. Michaels." After withdrawing the force, the barges commenced a bombardment of the town and the fire was strongly returned by guns on Mill Point and Impey Dawson's wharf. Only a few buildings were hit in roof and gable—including the well-known"CannonballHouse"—and there were no American injuries.

While the skirmish at St. Michaels might not be considered much of a battle by some, it saved the town and the shipyards. It further provided a controversy for the next two generations that enlivened and polarized local society. A few days after the battle, the county newspaper reported that one unit of militia ("Hearts of Oak") had promptly marched in perfect order to Royal Oak upon hearing the alarm. The envious people of Easton long tended to snicker at the battle. Residents of St. Michaels claimed that upcounty militia turned and ran at the sound of the first shot. Bloodshed in saloons far exceeded that of the two British marines in August, 1813.

RASPBERRY FOOL

During the summer of 1813 while county militia was quartered in St. Michaels expecting a British attack, the soldiers barracked in the town's two churches and stood their formations and prepared meals on the green of St. Mary's Square. It was a favorite pastime of the townsfolk, especially the young boys, to gather and watch the various activities. No menus survive, but a typical camp meal of that era consisted of fried beans and what later came to be called johnnycake, cooked on open fires.

With raspberries in season, the town that "fooled" the British that August night could have celebrated their victory with Raspberry Fool, an old English delicate and delicious dessert of fruit purée folded into thick cream or custard.

Reputedly fired by the British in the battle of St. Michaels.

1 quart raspberries, cleaned
1 cup sugar
3 cups heavy cream
1-1/2 teaspoons vanilla

In a large saucepan over low heat cook fruit 30 minutes; stir and mash pulp occasionally. Blend in sugar until dissolved. Process in blender or food processor; force through a sieve to eliminate seeds, if desired. Refrigerate until ready to serve.

In large bowl whip cream with vanilla until stiff peaks form. Gently fold in raspberry puree. Do not overblend; mixture should have a marbled effect. Serve in clear parfait glasses or individual dessert bowls.

•Sharp's Island

Sharp's Island Light—
Undermined by ice in recent years, the precarious light, photographed in 1988, is all that remains to mark the shoal of what was once Sharp's Island.

A former resident who witnessed the demise of Sharp's Island at the hands of the elements recalled:

"The worst storm was called the Centennial Storm because it occurred in the year of the exposition in Philadelphia (1876). We stood on our porch and watched the waves smashing over the pine trees, and the tide got so high it ran through a ditch and cut the island in two. We were there four winters, and in two of them Father was cut off from us on the mainland by the ice. We lived on goose soup or turkey soup for many a day."

Sharp's Island Hotel—*The three-story, six-gabled, thirty-room hotel built on the island in the late 1800s, doomed to extinction before it was built.*

Within the borders of Talbot County near the mouth of the Choptank River, Sharp's Island in 1660 comprised 700 acres. Farmland rich as well as a gunning and fishing paradise, it was also a popular cruising destination for many years. At the turn of the century the Alfretta Fishing Club was active on the island, described by one of its members as "bound on the north by soft crabs, on the east by fresh fish, on the south by mosquitos, and on the west by all three combined. It was originally a part of the mainland which blew into the Bay. . . ."

By 1848 Sharp's Island had been reduced by the strong tidal currents of the Choptank and the winds and storms of the Chesapeake to 438 acres. Fifty-two years later it had diminished to 91 acres. Though most of the island was still farmed as late as 1916, a good part of it disappeared in a vicious storm in August 1933. It came to an ignominious end as a bombing practice target during World War II.

STRAWBERRY CREAM ON A MERINGUE ISLAND

At one time the Delmarva Peninsula was the largest grower of strawberry plants in the world, as well as the largest shipping point for them. Strawberries blended with whipped cream atop a meringue base combine in this elegant, but easy, dessert spectacular.

MERINGUE
6 egg whites
1-1/2 cups sugar
1 teaspoon vinegar

STRAWBERRY CREAM FILLING
1 pint strawberries, washed, hulled, and sliced
    (additional strawberries for garnish)
1/3 cup sugar
1 pint heavy cream, whipped
1 teaspoon vanilla

Grease a 9-inch spring form pan; set aside.   Oven 325°

Meringue: In a large bowl beat egg whites until foamy; gradually add sugar a tablespoon at a time. Beat until sugar is dissolved and soft peaks form; beat in vinegar. Turn into greased pan; spread smooth. Bake for one hour; place on wire rack to cool. (Center of meringue will drop.) When cool, remove sides of pan and fill center with strawberry filling.

Strawberry Cream Filling: Combine strawberries and sugar; set aside. In a large bowl whip cream; fold in strawberries. Garnish with strawberries.

THE POPLAR ISLANDS

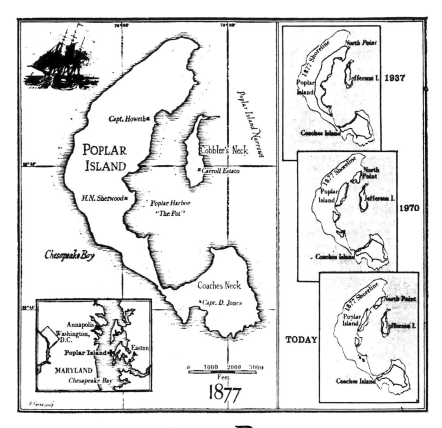

Belying their quiet and peaceful appearance today, the Poplar Islands have been the scene of several dramatic—indeed, very violent—events in history. After Captain William Claiborne became the first Englishman to settle with his family in Talbot County, a bloody Indian massacre nearly put an end to colonization. Later, during the War of 1812, the British attacked the islands, plundering as they went.

In the relatively calm years between 1880 and 1920, about 15 families enjoyed community life on the islands, which boasted productive farmlands, tobacco barns, a sawmill, schoolhouse, post office, and general store. By 1929, however, the islands had been taken over by moonshiners. In a raid later that year, revenuers made five arrests and smashed a 1,000-gallon still.

All during these tumultuous years, the Poplar Islands were washing away. Centuries of uncontrolled erosion ravaged their shores as they were battered by relentless winds and waves. Torn by the elements, the land was reduced from a single 1,000-acre island during colonial times to seven smaller islands by 1980. All that remains of these islands will eventually sink like Atlantis into a watery grave.

One of the more colorful chapters of life on the Poplar Islands occurred in the years from 1931 to 1946 when famous Democrats journeyed to the islands for rest and relaxation at their exclusive retreat, The Jefferson Islands Club, Inc.

Over the years these islands have been bought by different organizations which attempted to use them as hunting grounds. They were finally given to the Smithsonian Institution's Bay Center, which today utilizes their remains as a wildlife sanctuary and laboratory.

TILGHMAN ISLAND

Knapps Narrows, Tilghman Island

To describe it as approximately three miles long, three quarters of a mile wide, located at the southern end of Talbot County, and connected to the mainland by a drawbridge at Knapps Narrows does not begin to characterize Tilghman Island. The unique essence and identity of Tilghman is revealed in the people who live and work there.

Hardworking and independent, the Tilghman Islander typifies the Eastern Shoreman, almost an endangered species, caught as he is between poor seafood harvests in recent years and limitations placed on hunting (bag) limits. He is both the inimitable waterman and the avid hunter, especially savoring wild ducks and the Canada geese that winter on the Eastern Shore. Inhabiting one of the most important water communities on the Chesapeake Bay, the waterman's (and waterwoman's) heritage is legendary.

As an important boatbuilding center of Chesapeake Bay work craft for more than a century, Tilghman Island is considered home of Maryland's State Boat, the oyster dredging skipjack, said to be "skippered by men born without fear of man, God or the devil himself." An oysterman's trade requires Herculean strength in maneuvering the dredges, which can weigh up to 800 pounds when full. Endurance against the elements challenges the know-how of these hardiest of souls in an often brutal and dangerous job.

Historically, Tilghman Island has had a checkered past, consisting of small farms and large tomato and herring roe canneries. It has been, and still is, a busy shipping point for fish, oysters, and crabs. A Tilghman Islander's pride of place is perhaps best captured in the words of a bumper sticker proliferating on the Eastern Shore today— "There is no life west of the Chesapeake Bay." Tilghman Island is an enigma, unique unto itself as home port to flotillas of work boats and one of the largest skipjack fleets on the Bay, as well as being a sport fisherman's paradise— a place where boats have right of way.

Soft Shell Crabs

Preferred by many crab connoisseurs, the soft shell crab is a crab in its most vulnerable stage of life. Having burst its former hard shell and replaced it with a soft and tender one, it becomes prey for man and beast alike.

Soft shell crab season begins when the locust trees bloom in late May, and continues all summer long. Eastern Shore natives have traditionally served the crabs with the tender wild asparagus shoots that grow along the shoreline. Accompanied by fresh-baked bread and butter, it is a meal of incomparable delight.

Whether dredged lightly in flour and sautéed in nothing but butter, or deep fried or baked, these savory morsels often surprise the first-time taster, since they resemble large fried spiders. The following method of preparation comes from a native Tilghman Islander.

Prepare only live crabs. With a sharp paring knife, lift the top shell on each end and **remove the lungs** (grey and finger-shaped gills known as "dead man's fingers"). **Cut out the eyes** and pull off the apron (abdominal area) on the lower back shell. Rinse.

In a heavy skillet, preferably cast iron, place one tablespoon of vinegar and enough water to equal 1/4-inch depth. Put in crabs; season with salt and pepper to taste. Add about three tablespoons solid vegetable shortening. Cover and steam over medium heat until crabs turn red and are tender when pricked with a fork. Remove lid and brown quickly on each side.

EASTERN SHORE INDIANS·———————

Cakes of crab and a legacy of corn

Indians inhabiting the shores of the Great Shellfish Bay, the Chesapeake, gave tribal names to the rivers along which they lived—the Nanticokes, "they who ply the tidewater stream," and the Choptanks, "it flows back strongly." Manitou, the Indians' Great Power, provided varieties of seafood in endless quantities and an existence virtually free of hardship.

Diamondback terrapin and sea turtles were prized by the Indians for their meat as well as for their eggs. They also feasted on lobsters, and clams, and the plentiful oysters and crabs. Weirs—stake fences driven into river bottoms—trapped many varieties of fish, including white and yellow perch, rockfish,

In *Chesapeake*, James Michener describes 16th century crab cakes prepared by Navitan, a Nanticoke woman whose mother's recipe had been handed down to her:

"But when she took this meat, as her mother had taught her, and mixed it with herbs and vegetables and corn meal, and formed it into small cakes and fried them in sizzling bear fat, she produced one of the finest dishes this river would ever know. 'Cakes of Crab,' she called them, and Pentaquod found them subtle and delicious."

drum, roach, catfish, pike, trout, sheepshead, sturgeon, herring, and shad.

The fields and forests of Talbot County were such superior hunting and trapping grounds that they inspired territorial feuds between tribes. Many a hunting expedition followed paths which still exist as roads in the county today, and the Indians' prowess as hunters and trappers is legendary. They stalked small game such as rabbit, squirrel, opossum, and raccoon and otter, mink, and beaver were trapped in snares made of thongs so as not to ruin the pelts with arrow holes. Beaver tail was considered one of the finest of delicacies. Deer and bear were sought not only for their meat, but for skins which were fashioned into mantles and blankets. For a change of diet, Indians hunted ducks, geese, and swans in season.

Fire and corn were gods worshipped by the Indians. As a gift from the Great Spirit, corn was seen as the sustainer of life and played a pivotal role in religious observances and elaborate rituals. Throughout the region's history, cornbread and other corn dishes figured prominently as a diet staple.

With abundance everywhere from field, forest, and stream, Eastern Shore Indians had only to gather, cure, and store provisions for use during harsher months of the year. In addition to food preservation, Indians' skills and techniques, some of which survive today, recall their ability as boat builders and planters. They were also the first to use decoys in hunting waterfowl and tongs for harvesting oysters.

CORN MEAL PANCAKES

More than three centuries after it was founded, the Old Wye Mill in northern Talbot County still operates. The following recipe, passed down from Civil War times, is the Wye Miller's favorite. The pancakes are described as flavorful, nourishing, and easy to prepare.

1 cup corn meal
2 tablespoons sugar
1 teaspoon salt
1 cup boiling water
1 egg
2 tablespoons melted butter
1/2 cup milk
1/2 cup flour
2 teaspoons baking powder

In a large mixing bowl, combine corn meal, sugar, salt, and boiling water; let stand for 10 minutes. Beat egg, butter, and milk together; add to corn meal mixture. Sift flour and baking powder; add to batter. Bake on both sides on hot griddle.

Recipe courtesy of Barton McGuire, Miller—Old Wye Mill Society for the Preservation of Maryland Antiquities

THE GASTRONOMIC· EARLY SETTLER

An English traveler who visited Talbot County in 1705 wrote of a bear hunt and the feast which followed. "Some was Roasted some Boyled some Broyled ... I thought it as good as Roast Beefe it being very juicey and harty food full of gravey." The same man dined on "the great fox squirrel (Delmarva Fox Squirrel) ... rare good meat when boiled with a bit of bacon." He did, however, disdain the American rabbit which he thought skimpy compared to the English hare. Fish eaten by this Englishman included white and yellow perch, rockfish, catfish, drum, sheepshead, eels, herring, shad, and sturgeon. He especially liked the big sea turtles and oysters "big as horses hooves."

The early settlers developed a fondness for sassafras tea. Tons of the root were exported to England, and in bad years for tobacco, planters complained that sassafras root was the only crop they could sell. Wild fruit included persimmon, chestnuts, cherries, blackberries, quinces, and plums. Raising sheep was a problem because of the many wolves, but cattle and hogs flourished. Everybody had chickens, and the waterfowl that thrive today were hunted for food, with canvasback (duck) the epicure's choice. Wild turkeys went to any who were skillful enough to bring them down. Raccoon and opossum were considered delicacies while deer were so plentiful that venison became a "tiresome meat." A hogshead of sotweed (tobacco) procured all the table luxuries that gun and rod did not.

In the early years, political rallies were a popular pastime, drawing thousands of spectators. Fish feasts brought the people in to hear the speeches. Rallies were staged in groves by the water where seineloads of perch, drum, and rock were hauled in, cleaned, and fried on open fires. Oysters by the barrel were washed down with liberal quantities of hard cider, applejack, rum, and whiskey. As fish became more scarce, politicians substituted first hams and then whole oxen for feasts much like the bull roasts we have today.

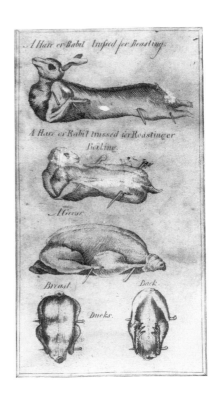

TO ROAST RABBITS

From *The Frugal Housewife*, or *Complete Woman Cook*, 1802:

"Baste them with good butter, and dredge them with a little flour. Half an hour will do them, at a very clear, quick fire, and if they are very small, twenty minutes will do them. Take the livers, with a little bunch of parsley and boil them, and then chop them very fine together. Melt some good butter, and put half the liver and parsley into the butter; pour it into the dish, and garnish the dish with the other half. Let the rabbits be done of a fine, light brown."

THE HAMBLETONS OF TALBOT COUNTY

Portrait of Samuel Hambleton as a young man (1806); crayon by Charles Fevret de Saint Memin (1770–1852).

Lake Erie seems far removed from the small Eastern Shore town of St. Michaels. But on the morning of September 10, 1813, at the height of the War of 1812, an event occurred which would forever tie these two parts of the country together.

On that day on Lake Erie an American fleet under the command of Commodore Oliver Hazard Perry scored a decisive victory over a numerically larger British force. With Perry on his flagship *Lawrence* was a 36-year-old purser, Samuel Hambleton, of St. Michaels. Samuel distinguished himself by helping to man one of the guns, and was severely wounded when a cannonball dropped from the rigging.

He survived and was soon well enough to write to his mother in St. Michaels describing the battle. That letter and a piece of his broken shoulder blade became treasured family heirlooms which were given to the Chesapeake Bay Maritime Museum.

Samuel Hambleton was perhaps the most outstanding member of one of Talbot County's oldest and most distinguished families. Samuel's great-great grandfather, William, arrived in Maryland in 1657. Two years later he received a patent for 200 acres near St. Michaels that became "Martingham," the family

seat, and remained so until 1945.

Over the years the Hambleton name became well known in the fields of agriculture, politics, business, and law. Samuel Hambleton's father, William, great-grandson of the first William, distinguished himself in the Revolutionary War as a captain of militia. Captain Hambleton and wife, Nancy Needles Hambleton, had 11 children, of which purser Hambleton was second oldest.

Samuel was born at Martingham in 1777 and served for a time as a merchant's clerk. In 1806, he was commissioned into the fledgling American Navy, as purser (or paymaster, as the rank was later entitled), and was initially stationed at New Orleans. In 1812 he was transferred to Newport, Rhode Island where he and Oliver Hazard Perry became close friends. When Perry was ordered to Lake Erie to take charge of the American squadron, Hambleton accompanied him at his friend's request. It was Hambleton who had the famous flag made which flew during the Battle of Lake Erie, emblazoned with Captain Lawrence's dying words, "Don't Give Up The Ship."

Samuel Hambleton made the Navy his career and remained on the active list until his death in 1851. His younger brother, John, followed him into the Navy, also as purser. When the brothers were not away on Navy business they resided at "Perry Cabin" on the outskirts of St. Michaels. Hambleton had purchased the 175-acre estate in 1812 for $2,808, and named it after his good friend and mentor. Perry Cabin was described in the 19th century as having "... rooms ... mostly large and airy, plainly furnished and devoid of ornament, except such as was given by the curious objects of nature and art brought from foreign parts."

Acknowledged mistress of the house was Lydia Hambleton, who, with her sister, Louisa, lived in Perry Cabin with brothers Samuel and John. Ample fireplaces took the chill off the long winters, while shade trees gave "delicious coolness to the summer air that came salt-laden across the lawn that sloped to the water's edge." Surrounding fields and orchards provided much food for the table.

Samuel took a keen interest in the farm and was a member of the Maryland Agricultural Society of the Eastern Shore. In later years he was inclined to portliness, with a ruddy complexion and a full head of white hair. His stern expression and heavy eyebrows belied a reputation for kindness to children, although he had none of his own, preferring to remain a bachelor.

Perry Cabin went out of the family in 1904. Later, in the 1920's, under the ownership of Charles H. Fogg, the house sustained considerable remodeling. Recently, it was further modified to become a restaurant and inn and is no longer the simple and unadorned structure of Samuel Hambleton's time.

HAMBLETON CAKE

A July, 1905 entry in a private journal discovered at the Talbot County Historical Society contained this recipe for Hambleton Cake. It is presented here exactly as scripted and, as in the tradition of the best cooks, much is "understood," not only in the method of preparation, but in amounts of ingredients required.

The expression in the recipe "until it ropes" is used in candy-making to describe the consistency of a water/sugar syrup which should become ropelike and sticky. A cookbook published in the mid-1800's described this stage: "In putting a spoon into the syrup, when drawing it out, a long thread of sugar will follow the spoon."

5 eggs
1/2 pound butter
2 cups sugar
1 cup milk
1 teaspoon soda
2 teaspoons cream of tartar
4 cups flour

Use the whites of two eggs for icing with 2 cups sugar, boiled until it ropes—then pour on whites, beat until cold—flavor with almond, cake and icing.

27

FREDERICK DOUGLASS

Orator, Abolitionist, Statesman

Frederick Douglass was born Frederick Bailey in 1817, a slave, at Holme Hill Farm on Tuckahoe Creek. His maternal ancestry traced back to the earliest arrivals in America, and his physical appearance suggested Indian bloodlines. It was suspected his father was a white man.

At age six, he was sent to Wye House to serve as a companion-servant to 12-year-old Daniel Lloyd. As a house slave he gained insights into society as well as absorbing some of the education given to Daniel.

Upon the death of Aaron Anthony, his original owner, he became the property of Thomas Auld of St. Michaels, who sent him to serve his brother in Baltimore. Although a slave, he lived a relatively "free" life, and was allowed to learn and participate in neighborhood activities.

When he was recalled to St. Michaels, Thomas Auld felt Frederick was too arrogant and sent him to Edward Covey, a "slave breaker" who operated a farm near Wade's Point in Bay Hundred. It was there as a field hand that Frederick was beaten and whipped. Later he would show the scars on his back to audiences, declaring they were his authority to denounce slavery.

His next assignment was to William Freeland, whose farm was adjacent to Martingham on the Miles River. It was here he conducted a clandestine school for the Blacks of the area. After being caught in an escape attempt in 1836, Auld sent him back to Baltimore. He would not return for 41 years.

1838 was Frederick's year of decisive action. He escaped to the North, changed his name to Douglass, sent for and married Anna Murray

Believed to have belonged to the sister of Frederick Douglass, Eliza Bailey Mitchell, Mitchell House was saved from demolition and moved to the Chesapeake Bay Maritime Museum. The original portion of the house on the left was typical of the 19th century southern Maryland Black tenant house. This humble, circa 1830 two-story cabin was formerly part of the Perry Cabin Farm plantation owned by John Needles Hambleton.

In his *Life of an American Slave*, Douglass reported that, as part of their monthly allowance, slaves were given eight pounds of pork, or its equivalent in fish, and one bushel of corn meal. Upon returning to St. Michaels on June 17, 1877 after a life of accomplishment, Frederick Douglass, the most famous Black man in the world at that time, addressed a mixed audience of Blacks and Whites:

"I'm an Eastern Shoreman with all that that name implies, Eastern Shore corn and Eastern Shore pork gave me my muscle. I love Maryland and the Eastern Shore."

BAKED PORK CHOPS WITH APPLES

6 thick pork chops
Salt to taste
6 tart apples—peel, core and slice 1-inch thick
1/4 cup water
1/4 cup sugar

Oven 350°   6 Servings

In a greased skillet brown pork chops on both sides. While chops are browning, prepare apples. Reserving pan juices, remove chops to a casserole which will accommodate chops in one layer. Sprinkle with salt. Add water to skillet, scraping sides and bottom; pour over chops. Arrange apple slices on top of chops; sprinkle with sugar. Cover and bake 45 minutes to 1 hour until chops are tender.

BAKED CORN

2 eggs, beaten
1 cup sugar
2 tablespoons corn starch
1/4 teaspoon salt
2 cups fresh corn or 1 16-ounce can cream style
    white corn
Scant tablespoon vanilla
2-1/4 cups milk

Preheat Oven to 450°   10 to 12 Servings

In large mixing bowl combine all ingredients. Grease a two-quart casserole; place corn mixture in casserole. Bake at 450° about 25 to 30 minutes or until top browns; reduce heat to 400°. Bake 30 to 45 minutes until set. Serve hot or cold.

from the Eastern Shore, and began his abolitionist activities in earnest. A lecturer and author, he wrote *Narrative of My Experiences in Slavery* in 1844, and *My Bondage and My Freedom* in 1855. A publisher of many abolitionist tracts, he was one of the leaders of the slave underground network.

As his career burgeoned, he was nominated for vice president and later became United States Marshal for the District of Columbia, as well as its Recorder of Deeds. Abraham Lincoln appointed him Minister and Consul General to Haiti. In his later years, Douglass served as presidential advisor to several administrations.

Frederick Douglass died in the District of Columbia on February 20, 1895. He is buried in Rochester, New York. His name was given to the elementary school that served the Black children of the St. Michaels and Bay Hundred districts of Talbot County prior to the opening of the larger, integrated St. Michaels Elementary-Middle School. The primary wing of the newer school currently carries his name.

A State Roads Commission historical marker on the Easton-Denton Road (route 328), west of the Tuckahoe River Bridge, recognizes his birth on Tuckahoe Creek, and a marker at Mill and Talbot Streets in St. Michaels encapsulates his life story.

SCHOOL DAYS CHRONICLE

In colonial times it was the young white male only who received an education. While some of the wealthy were sent to European schools, the majority were taught by indentured men teachers. Sometimes groups of students from several plantations would combine in what were known as "subscription schools," which were actually the first private schools in America.

In Talbot County, the earliest institutional school was located about halfway between Easton and St. Michaels in 1727. Known as the Talbot County Free School, it was operated by the St. Peters (Easton) and St. Michaels Parishes, offering a curriculum of "grammar, good writing, and mathematics." After it burned in 1780, the land was sold and the proceeds were used to help found Washington College in Chestertown, the first college established in Maryland and one of the oldest in America.

Private family schools continued to provide most of the education. In 1834, with the passage of "Spencer's School Law," (calling for public education for Whites only), elementary schoolhouses opened in every village and hamlet in the county. Girls were permitted to attend, but most stayed home to receive domestic and social training. The first St. Michaels schoolhouse, established in 1835, was in the Market House on

St. Mary's Square. By 1856 the county had 42 school districts and 50 teachers.

The St. Michaels Female Academy opened in an abandoned church on St. Mary's Square in 1857. It closed when the county offered public secondary education to girls. After the Civil War there were several new private schools, but the St. Michaels Classical and Mathematical Academy, the St. Michaels Private School, and the Girls Academy of Royal Oak were all short-lived.

Before the Emancipation Proclamation in 1863 there was no education for Blacks unless it was obtained secretly. Black education was limited to a few classes conducted by some of their

Portico of St. Mary's Square Grammar School, circa 1908. The stately building was fatefully destroyed by fire in the 1940's.

31

churches. In 1865 Lewis Douglass was frustrated in his attempt to start a school for Blacks at Ferry Neck (Bellevue). He wrote to his father, the celebrated Frederick Douglass, about the difficulty of the experience.

In the early 1900's schools for Blacks were opened around the county, but only up to the seventh grade; there was no secondary education for Blacks until 1937. Until then, some church-sponsored youths were sent to Princess Anne where there was a church academy. Others moved in with relatives living where there were Black high schools.

The first county White high school opened in 1886, serving only the Easton area. St. Michaels High followed by 1900, and Tilghman High in 1916. During this period there were 70 county schools, 51 of which were the one-room type.

With the establishment of a county bus system in 1917, many small schools were consolidated with larger community schools. Tilghman High closed in 1930 and students were bused to a newly-built high school in St. Michaels.

Moton High School for Black students opened in Easton in 1937, eventually reaching a peak enrollment of 900 students from throughout the county. A new Moton was built in 1953, as well as Frederick Douglass Elementary School in St. Michaels, which replaced the remaining Black schools in Bay Hundred. These schools operated under the philosophy of "separate but equal" education for three years, at which time the student was free to choose his or her school. With the advent of integration, Moton students were transferred to either Easton High or St. Michaels High Schools. Frederick Douglass Elementary School closed when the new St. Michaels Elementary-Middle School was built. Complete desegregation was effected by 1966.

SCHOOL LUNCH MENU OF OLD

In *Some Random Recollections of My First Year of Teaching* (September, 1920), Mary F. Clough, a young woman of 17, recorded her experiences in a one-room country schoolhouse on the St. Michaels Road. Among her memoirs was a notation that, "Lunches were brought from home and were lined up on a shelf for the noon break. They carried tin pails or leather buckets."

In addition to the three R's, this special teacher taught life's lessons of sharing, teamwork, and the fellowship of food. By making use of the central potbellied stove, soup was occasionally prepared before nine o'clock and simmered all morning. The teacher provided a large kettle and spoon as well as the meat. Children contributed whatever they could bring from home—ingredients such as potatoes, cabbage, onions, turnips, and beans. As a special treat on cold days, the teacher brought cocoa and sugar for hot cocoa. In these demonstrations of genuine caring, this kind woman exemplified the dedication often attributed to members of the teaching profession.

For generations, peanut butter has been a favorite among youngsters. With only four ingredients, Lunch Bucket Peanut Butter cookies are super easy, super fast, and super good. The raw dough is so tasty, better double the recipe.

1 cup peanut butter
1 cup sugar
1 egg
1 teaspoon vanilla

Oven 325°   Yield: About 24

In a large bowl combine peanut butter and sugar. Add egg and vanilla; mix well. With palms of hands, roll dough into balls about the size of a small walnut. Place on lightly greased baking sheets. Flatten balls with fork tines, crisscross fashion. Bake 13–15 minutes; cool slightly before removing from baking sheet.

VICTUALLING· THE SAILOR

Historically, food aboard ship was very substantial and the amplitude of the meals more than made up for the lack of variety. While the victualling of a ship was usually contracted for, the captain was nonetheless faced with major problems. Supplies, when sent aboard, were often spoiled and of poor quality. Greed on the part of the victualler, or chandler, was flagrant and often the ship would be at sea before the misrepresentation was discovered.

One of the earliest victualling laws was the British Admiralty's requirement in 1545 that every seaman be issued daily a pound of biscuit, a pound of salted meat, and a gallon of beer. The salted meat could be replaced three days a week by a pound of cheese and a dried fish.

During Admiral Nelson's time, rations per man were increased to include a weekly two pints of peas, three pints of oatmeal, eight ounces of butter, and a pound of cheese. In place of the gallon of beer, which spoiled quickly, a pint of rum was issued. In 1795 the Admiralty ordered a daily issue of lemon juice to every sailor, mixed with the rum ration to ensure that it would be consumed. Ten years later,

scurvy had almost been abolished in the British Navy.

By 1890, there was also a small allotment of tea, coffee, and sugar and a daily issue of lime juice. This daily issue of lime juice gave the British their nickname, "limeys."

Every variation of food had its own special name. Ship's biscuits, called "hard tack" or "pantiles" by the sailors, had the texture of a dog biscuit and were inedible unless soaked in water. For breakfast, the crew usually had broken pieces of biscuit boiled in water and mixed with leftover bits of salt beef, pork scraps, or anything handy in the galley. This "lobscouse," or cracker stew, was baked in the oven and developed a crisp top. As a special treat, the cook would sometimes pour a ladle full of sorghum or blackstrap molasses on top of the baked stew, which would then be called "dandyfunk."

"Plum duff," a Sunday special, was made by pounding biscuits to a powder in a canvas bag. Currants, raisins, jams, and pieces of pork fat would be added, the bag tied off, and thrown into a pot of boiling water. The pudding that was the final product was usually the only indication that Sunday had arrived.

Salt beef and pork came

aboard ships in the 1800s in 300-pound casks. The meat had been previously saturated in brine and then packed tight and dry with saltpeter in the casks. The salt beef was justifiably referred to by sailors as "salt horse," even though a sufficient soaking time was allowed to remove most of the salt.

Fresh water at sea was always limited. Clothing washed in salt water and being continuously salted down on the outside as well gave rise to the sailor's nickname, "old salt." Stored water, especially in the tropics, became stagnant and unpalatable very quickly. Rum punch, or "grog"—the sailors' favorite for over 400 years—is said to have originated among English sailors in about 1552 and consisted of a simple mixture of cane spirits and sugar, heated.

The evening issuance of rum was abolished in 1824 and the total ration reduced to one gill (10 ounces U.S. measure) of rum in 1850. Grog derived its name from the nickname of Admiral Sir Edward Vernon, called "old grog," in allusion to his wearing a grogram cloak and britches. Lawrence Washington, half brother of George Washington, named his estate, Mt. Vernon, for this Admiral under whom he had served.

In order to combat drunkenness among seamen, Vernon issued an order in 1740 that the daily pint issue of rum be divided and served twice a day, one half at noon and the other half at six o'clock. A ballad commemorates the occasion:

A mighty bowl on deck he drew
And filled it to the brink
Such drank the Burford's
gallant crew
And such the gods shall drink.
The sacred robe
which Vernon wore
Was drenched with the same:
And hence its virtues
guard our shore
And grog derives its name.

"Old Salt"
Captain John F. Berridge of Tilghman Island, waterman and pound net fisherman.

WATERMEN

They Follow the Water

The classic picture of a waterman is that of a solitary figure in the morning mist, tonging for oysters or running his trotline, independent and self-reliant. Indeed, in the 1860s actual battles—the so-called Oyster Wars—were fought and watermen were killed in territorial disputes. Long known for his resistance to authority, the waterman to this day looks upon the Department of Natural Resources and its rules as merely a necessary evil.

Since the 1950s the number of watermen on the Bay has declined. High maintenance costs for work boats and equipment, and decreasing income, have made other vocations more attractive to many of the younger men.

Fifty and more years ago a visitor from outside the Chesapeake Bay area could tour its waterfront communities and have difficulty understanding much of what the residents were saying since many of their pronunciations, special words and expressions were unique. Each area had its different accent and colloquialisms.

Now, however, only the old-timers speak in any singular way.

"If you ain't been aground, you ain't been nowhere . . . if you're lookin' for somethin' in a fog and you git there and it ain't, damn it, you're lost"

"Hark and understand what I say. I might learn you something"

Watermen can be found only in the Chesapeake Bay area. They make their living on and from the water. Folk on other waters also tong and dredge oysters, work trotlines and crab pots, dig for clams, fish, and hunt. They are referred to by their local names, like baymen, fishermen, or boatmen. Only on the Chesapeake are they called "watermen."

"You got to be born on the water, to do anything on the water"

Most watermen can trace their families living on the Bay and its waters for generations. Some go back to the 1600s when the Indians taught the colonists how to harvest the Bay. Rarely did a waterman move far from where he was born.

"All of 'ems got it, none'll admit it"

Whichever method was used, old watermen could be spotted by their hands, which would be scarred and discolored from oyster shell cuts, a condition known as 'arster hand.' Not so easy to see was the numbness and soreness in their fingers, hands, and arms, known as 'tongers disease.'

"It war a kind o' oozy, easy bottom; a little cindery but no' 'sactly. We moved to the hard but they war scase, too"

Isolated until the Bay Bridge and connecting roads were built, speech changed little from the earliest days. Since much Old English was mixed with the special colloquialisms of each particular area, strangers found it difficult to understand what was being said. With the expansion of communication, the watermen's uniqueness of speech is gradually disappearing and speech alone no longer identifies a waterman.

SUPERSTITION

Things that can bring bad luck on a work boat:

- anything blue
- three crows flying across a boat's bow
- a hatch cover up-side down

- using a red brick as ballast
- having a leaf, nut or twig from a walnut tree on board
- allowing a woman on board
- changing the name of a boat

"The only resource that's any good to you is the one in the boat"

While watermen can do anything on the water (and land), there are basically two seasons. Oysters when it's cool or cold; crabs when it's warm or hot.

"An arster makes a clam taste common"

Methods of harvesting oysters divide watermen into hand tongers, patent tongers, dredgers (pronounced 'drudgers'), and, recently, divers.

"If these science fellers are right, we got a lot to learn 'bout arsters"

The oyster industry was at its peak at the turn of the century, involving over 7,000 watermen, as well as 10,000 others in related land operations. At one time there were over 2,000 vessels "drudgin' the rocks." By 1966 only 67 skipjacks remained to dredge Maryland's waters. Since then, the number of skipjacks working the Bay has steadily declined.

"Use to be a man could walk across (the cove) on the workboats. Won't never be no more"

DREDGE BOAT STEW

Historically, meals aboard dredge boats and other work boats were, of necessity, hearty and substantial. Early morning workdays were fortified with the ubiquitous coffeepot and ample breakfasts. The strength and endurance required by crew members were sustained by stick-to-the-ribs cooking. Freshly baked bread or biscuits were staples, along with hearty bean soups and stews. Fried chicken, french fried potatoes, cracker pudding, fried bean fritters, dried fruits, and corned beef occasionally appeared on galley tables.

6 strips bacon
1 medium onion, chopped
3 medium potatoes, peeled and cubed
3 cups water
1 pint oysters in their liquor
Salt and pepper to taste
Tabasco to taste

In large saucepan fry bacon, reserving drippings; drain; crumble, and set aside. Sautée onion in bacon drippings; add potatoes and water. Simmer until potatoes just begin to disintegrate. Mash a few potatoes against side of pot to thicken stew. Add crumbled bacon and oysters with liquor; cook until edges of oysters curl. Season to taste with salt, pepper, and tabasco. Serves 4.

37

OYSTER HARVESTING

Dredging *("drudgin' ")—Iron dredges are thrown overboard and dragged along river bottoms to scoop the oysters. At first, aided only by the boat's winches, the dredges were hoisted by the sheer brute strength of crew members. Later, as the gasoline engine was developed, it's power was utilized to raise the heavy dredges to the side of the boat.*

Sloops and schooners were the first oyster dredge boats. Now the work is done exclusively by skipjacks. By law, the boats must work under sail only (except on Mondays and Tuesdays, when a yawl boat may be used to push).

Patent Tonging—*The mechanized tong, patented in 1887, is raised and lowered by cable and works deep-water oyster beds. Tongs are lowered, mechanically closed, and hoisted.*

Buy Boat—*Dredge boat crews often worked the oyster beds for weeks at a time. To ensure freshness, the oyster harvests were sold to "buy boat" crews who, in turn, transported the oysters to markets on the Bay.*

Hand Tonging—*Tongs, often weighing as much as 40 pounds, are lowered over the side of a work boat. The waterman closes the tongs on the oyster bed and raises the closed tongs hand-over-hand into the boat where the oysters are culled (sorted).*

Go 'Way

"Go 'Way" is a hearty codfish hash consisting of boiled potatoes in their skins, boiled codfish, crumbled bacon, raw or fried onions, and bacon drippings or butter. The name may be a derivation of County Galway in Ireland on Galway Bay. Dredge boat crews were said to complain if Go 'Way wasn't served by the cook.

To Prepare Salt Cod Soak cod eight hours or over night; wash under running water until free of saltiness; scald; simmer about one hour; boil five minutes; drain.

Ingredients are placed on galley tables in individual bowls. Each crew member prepares his plate by first mashing the potatoes; flaked codfish is layered over the potatoes (the codfish is prepared from dried salt cod that has been soaked for several hours to eliminate the salt and boiled in fresh water until it becomes dry and flaky). Bacon drippings or butter are drizzled over the mixture and topped by crumbled bacon and either fried or raw onions.

Leftover ingredients are made into codfish cakes for the next meal.

BULL LIPS, PIGS' EARS, AND EELS

The Waterman's Crab Bait

> C*rab Scraping*—The process of crab scraping is similar to oyster dredging and involves dragging a dredge in the Bay's shallows. The dredge is a metal frame without teeth and not as heavy as an oyster dredge. Crabs are forced into a net bag of sturdy twine mesh.

Crab Pot—*The crab pot is a cube-shaped trap typically made of galvanized chicken wire. An arched partition separates top from bottom; crabs are attracted to the bottom section by bait in the pot's center bait box. Having entered small openings in the pot's bottom section, the crab finds itself trapped and instinctively swims to the top of the trap.*

Crab Trotline—*A trotline is often half a mile long, or longer, and is baited every three to four feet with pieces of eel, bull lips, or pigs' ears. The ends are attached to buoys and the line lies along the bottom of the creek or river. One end of the line is lifted out of the water and placed on a roller. As the work boat moves along the trotline, the line is brought to the surface and moves through the roller. Crabs still feeding on the bait are netted out and sorted for size.*

EEL

The sadly misunderstood eel boasts a delicate, somewhat sweet flavor which is preferred by Eastern Shore Marylanders to the smoked eel more commonly found in urban markets. As with all fish cookery, freshness is paramount.

If you're not usin' him for bait, here's how to fix him. Chicken necks and fish heads are used (for bait) by weekend crabbers and tourists.

1 eel
Cold water
4–5 tablespoons salt
Seasonings to taste
Lemon juice
Butter

Nail the eel's head to a board. From its gills slit the skin around the circumference of the eel. With two pairs of pliers, one on each side of the eel, pull the skin off completely.

Slit the under-body and remove intestines; soak in container of cold salted water for two hours to draw out blood.

Fillet by cutting lengthwise and remove backbone. Cut into three-inch pieces; dispose of head.

Place eel pieces on a broiler pan lined with aluminum foil. Season to taste with onion salt, pepper, or other seasonings. Sprinkle with lemon juice; dot with butter.

Broil on lowest rack for about 20 minutes depending on thickness of eel. Meat will be flaky when pierced with fork.

41

THE LIFE (AND DEATH) OF A LIGHTKEEPER

Hooper Strait Lighthouse

From a letter dated May 31, 1971 by Jennie Bozman Alexander whose father drowned during his tenure as Lightkeeper.

My father, Calvin H. Bozman, was the lightkeeper of the Hooper Strait lighthouse in Dorchester County, Maryland for several years. This is the same lighthouse which you have moved to your Maritime Museum and restored there.

On September 4, 1918 he left home in Dames Quarter, Maryland and sailed to the lighthouse to relieve his partner, Mr. Ulman Owens, also of Dames Quarter. This was the last time my father was seen alive.

When the steamboat which ran between Baltimore and the lower Eastern Shore passed the Hooper Strait lighthouse, it was noticed that the light was not lit. This was, of course, reported as soon as the boat reached Baltimore, as this was before the days of radio. My father was found to be missing and presumed drowned, as there were indications he had fallen overboard. After a search, his body was recovered on September 7, 1918.

Each summer the keeper was allowed to take his family aboard the lighthouse for a week and we children looked forward to this visit each year, as we liked to go up and down the winding stairway and fish from the lighthouse. I remember that when a boat would pass the lighthouse my father would salute them by ringing the big bell.

Lighthouse keepers lived a hazardous and lonely life, especially in winter when the cold weather and freezing water made it almost impossible to leave the lighthouse. The keepers had to maintain the lighthouses inside and outside and they were kept busy in all weather scrubbing and waxing floors, shining brass locks, spigots on the water barrels, and all the other brass fixtures.

When I was in St. Michaels on Sunday, May 23rd, 1971, it was the first time I had seen the Hooper Strait lighthouse since my father had drowned, and many memories were brought back to me. Since I remember well how it all looked back then, I think you are to be congratulated for doing such a fine job in restoring it.

Yours, sincerely,

Jennie Bozman Alexander

DEVIL'S FOOD FOG· AND THE FRESNEL LENS

Lighthouses share a place in my earliest memories reserved by most children for teddy bears, favorite pets, and the laughter of friends. Our house stood alone and, in my darkened bedroom, nose pressed against the cold glass, I would watch a dozen twinkling lights beckoning the way to distant harbors. I soon learned to identify each lighthouse by its own distinctive blink, and if called upon to perform for company, my proud father had me recite not verses from Mother Goose, but the coded flashes of lighthouses guarding the seaway to our village.

But it was during the summer months that I really came to know my winter friends. My father enjoyed testing his piloting skills, and when we awoke to a real "pea soup" fog, my mother, without prompting, retired to the kitchen to produce her specialty, A CHOCOLATE LAYER CAKE OF SINFUL RICHNESS, while Dad busied himself with charts, tide tables, and dividers. With all in readiness we packed ourselves aboard our little launch, I perched in the bow peering pointlessly into the soft gray wall, my father at the tiller with stopwatch in hand, eyes glued to the compass, and Mother huddled under her raincoat, certain that *this* was the time we would miss our destination, not to be heard from until our withered remains drifted onto a European beach. She need not have worried; a gray-on-gray mosaic of broken rocks would eventually materialize, slowly followed by the base of the lighthouse they supported and protected from the tide-driven ice of winter. One of the younger keepers was always at hand to help make fast and to assist my mother, and the cake, ashore. I used to believe that he waited just for our arrival, and on these particular days perhaps he did; it is nice to think that "Devil's Food Fog" was an accepted addition to the local marine forecast.

Following admiration and sharing of the cake in the spotless kitchen, there would be a tour of the lighthouse for my reluctant benefit. Reluctant, because on foggy days it always included a visit to the room housing the fog horn mechanism. Close-up, these bellowing monsters had little in common with the distant lowing which lulled me to sleep on summer evenings, shaking a four-year-old with the force of an explosion, then stopping for breath while I cringed and flinched waiting for the next assault.

Augustin Fresnel, a French physicist, revolutionized the illumination of lighthouses worldwide with his invention of a lens that was able to direct light into a single beam by means of prisms. The Fresnel lens is made up of cut-glass prisms which reflect and refract light from the lamp. Here, the story is told of a young lad's fascination with lighthouses and his introduction to the awesome power of the Fresnel lens.

43

There was no such hesitancy, though, when time came to visit the lamp room, and I would gleefully scamper up the circular iron staircase to admire the big gleaming lenses in their polished brass mountings. Children are acutely attuned to the attitudes of the adults around them, and long before I learned the meaning of "dedication" I was aware that upon entering the lamp room these men and my father dropped their voices in respect, much as I had learned to do when entering church on Sunday mornings. Accompanied by unnecessary admonitions "not to touch," I would be balanced on the protective railing, admiring the lamp and its gauze-like mantle, and the inscription, "Paris, 1883." I assumed this to be the name of the land I could see across the Bay, having been assured it was on the other side of the ocean. Many years later I found that we were indebted to these prismatic Fresnel lenses for the warm and friendly glow of even our largest lighthouses, for in truth they did not make the soft light of the oil lamps brighter, only bigger, quite unlike the harshly brilliant pulses we owe to today's electronics.

Several years ago, cruising with a friend, I passed our lighthouse for the first time in almost 50 years. It was a forlorn sight, for like all lighthouses on the Bay, its keepers had long been gone, and it served now as no more than a support for a light and horn, and the electronics that directed them. Stains of rust and blistered paint scarred the tower, and the little rockbound cove where we used to go ashore harbored only graffiti and stranded beer cans.

I realize the Coast Guard has other priorities, and that it will eventually put another coat of paint on the aging structure, but I am glad none of the old Light House Service Inspectors is here to see this relic of a tradition where fresh paint and polish were a way of life. Undoubtedly, the modern lights are brighter, less expensive, and completely dependable, but machinery and electronics are a pale substitute for the reassuring presence of dedicated and capable men.

The Fresnel Lens
Fresnel lenses come in different "orders," or sizes. The largest is a first order; first and second order lenses are used at sea and are called "landfall lights." Third and fourth order lenses signal harbor entrances. Fifth and sixth order lenses mark rivers and channels.

The Hooper Strait Lighthouse, now at the Chesapeake Bay Maritime Museum, originally displayed a fourth order lens. This lens, exhibited on the second floor of the lighthouse, is a third order lens. A fifth order lens beams atop the lighthouse today.

CHOCOLATE CAKE

As dark and moist as fog, this cake from the Pettyjohn-DeHart family has been handed down for four generations. An old-fashioned loaf-style cake, the recipe is so tried and true it comes out perfectly every time. The cake may also be baked in a 9″×13″ sheet pan or in round layer-cake pans.

1/2 cup butter or margarine
1/2 cup baking cocoa
1-1/2 cups sugar
1 egg, beaten
1/2 cup buttermilk
2 teaspoons baking soda
2 cups flour
1 teaspoon baking powder
2 teaspoons vanilla
1 cup boiling water

Oven 350°

In a large mixing bowl, cream butter; add cocoa and sugar; cream together; beat in egg. Combine buttermilk and baking soda; beat into mixture. Blend in flour and baking powder, beat in vanilla. Lightly mix in boiling water until batter is smooth.

Grease and flour a large loaf pan (1-1/2 quart). Bake about one hour or until a toothpick inserted in center comes out clean. Cool in pan; remove when completely cooled. Frost with a 7-minute white or butter icing.

PENINSULA OF PLENTY

*Threshing Rig—Wyetown,
Talbot County*

If the Delmarva Peninsula—comprised of Delaware, Maryland, and Virginia—were larger, it would very likely compete with the West in the quantity and variety of crops it produces. The region boasts over 65 kinds of vegetables—everything from asparagus to zucchini; apple, peach, plum, cherry, and pear orchards, several varieties of melons and berries, acres of strawberry and blueberry fields, and persimmons, quince, grapes, and warm-climate figs. Blessed with the necessary rainfall, corn, soybeans, oats, rye, barley, and buckwheat, plus hay and forage crops are harvested with high bushels-per-acre yields. Pecan, hickory, and English and black walnut trees abound.

So impressed was an early colonist by this land of plenty that he wrote his friends in England, "... famine (the dreadful ghost of penury and want) is never known with his pale visage to haunt the

APPLESAUCE CAKE

The World War I era saw the rise of dairying and truck farming. Valerie Layman Youngs, one of six children who grew up on a 72-acre farm in Royal Oak, reminisces:

"We didn't have anything fancy, but everything was good. Just plain, country cooking. We grew or raised almost everything for the table. We canned fruits and vegetables, raised hogs, had a milk cow, and made our own butter. We canned pork, chicken, and the muskrats that my brother trapped. Sometimes we made cakes with duck eggs. We bartered for sugar with eggs, strawberries, or home made butter. Food was prepared using the old wood cookstove.

At Christmas-time, special treats were oranges, grapefruits, or dates stuffed with the black walnuts from trees on the farm. It wouldn't have been Christmas without applesauce cake. We made it ahead of time and it would keep for weeks if it was stored in a cool place because of the vinegar in it. The applesauce was made from apples in the orchard."

This recipe has been in Valerie Layman Youngs' family for several generations. It is chock-full of raisins and spices and should be baked in an old-fashioned tube pan. The aroma that permeates the air while the cake is baking gives pause to wonder how the cake survived weeks before Christmas with six children around.

1/2 cup solid vegetable shortening
1 cup brown sugar
2 cups flour
1/2 teaspoon salt
1 teaspoon cinnamon
1 teaspoon nutmeg
1 teaspoon powdered cloves
1 teaspoon baking soda
16 ounces applesauce
2 tablespoons cider vinegar
1 box (16 oz.) raisins

Oven 375°

Grease and flour tube cake pan.

In large mixing bowl cream shortening and brown sugar together. Sift all dry ingredients together and blend into creamed mixture. Add applesauce and vinegar; mix well. Add raisins and mix well.

Bake approximately one hour or until a broomstraw comes out clean.

dominions of Maryland."

In Talbot County, Tobacco ("sotweed") was king. Eventually, planters turned to wheat, corn, and other grains. The Revolutionary War could not have been won if farmers had not switched from growing tobacco to wheat. Wheat and flour were produced in such quantities on the Delmarva Peninsula that it became America's primary grain-growing region, known as "the breadbasket of the Revolution."

Maryland's Cannery Row

It may only be a footnote in American history, but it is nonetheless a fact that Admiral Richard E. Byrd took a good supply of Valliant's Canned Spinach with him on his expeditions to the South Pole. Said to have the "same health giving properties" as the oyster, spinach, as well as tomatoes and figs, were canned in large volume by the Valliant family from

VALLIANT PLANT AT BELLEVUE.
WHERE QUALITY REIGNS.

The Valliant packing plant, Bellevue, as it looked about 1914.

1895 through the 1940s. William H. Valliant, Sr., started his prosperous business with a "sanitary" oyster packing plant on the Tred Avon River at Bellevue across from Oxford, but later expanded this to include a cannery for which he grew his own crops. Cans were brought from var-

ious sources and the tops soldered by hand until around 1910, when Valliant added machinery to crimp the tops. Colorful labels were applied by hand.

At the turn of the century, canneries and seafood packing plants were prolific on both the eastern and western shores of Maryland. When World War I began there were 406 canneries in Maryland—the leading tomato canning state in the nation until the 1940s when the West Coast canning industry began to outpace the East, and Delmarva farmers began to receive better returns on chickens than on perishables. Today fewer than 15 canneries remain on Maryland's Eastern Shore, most of them canning tomatoes.

One of the largest canning operations on the Eastern Shore during the early 1900s was run by the Harrison and Jarboe families. At one point they owned eight canning and packing plants which processed fish, oysters, tomatoes, and clams. One of their sites, Navy Point, was acquired in 1910 from the St. Michaels Packing Company (owned by the Shannahan family) and is now occupied by the Chesapeake Bay Maritime Museum. Another bustling operation located at Navy Point was the Coulbourne and Jewett Seafood

Packing Company which packed and shipped thousands of barrels of crabs each year, as well as many tons of oysters. Frederick Jewett is credited with the idea of grading crabmeat according to backfin, special, regular, claw, and lump—classifications still in use today. His son, Elwood, took over the business in the 1940s when the firm was packing a million pounds of crab per year. Shortly after Elwood retired in 1965, the property was bought by the newly formed Maritime Museum.

The Tilghman (Island) Packing Company, in its heyday, annually prepared and shipped over 100,000 gallons of fresh oysters, several million hard crabs, five million herring, and 150,000 cases of corn and tomatoes. As late as 1960, this Harrison family enterprise was the largest seafood processor in Maryland—utilizing two large processing plants which stood on a man-made island of discarded oyster shells. The island, Avalon, is still there, but the packing plants have long since disappeared.

The St. Michaels and Bay Hundred districts of Talbot County were dominated by the canning industry during the early 20th century even though hours were long and wage levels low. Payment was often in the form of tokens, which could only be spent at the company store. Nevertheless, canning provided employment for many. As pickers, peelers, or packers they preserved the taste of Maryland for others. It is rumored that, even now, there are still a few cans of Valliant Spinach perfectly preserved at Byrd's South Pole outpost awaiting a hungry explorer.

Stewed Tomatoes

This typical Eastern Shore side dish is an old recipe originating many years ago on Tilghman Island. A cast iron skillet is absolutely essential in the preparation of these stewed tomatoes. There is nothing fancy about them—they're just good. Prepared in advance, they're even better.

1 small onion, finely chopped
3 tablespoons butter
1 28-ounce can whole tomatoes *or* 6 to 8 fresh
    tomatoes, peeled and chopped
1-1/4 teaspoons salt
1/2 teaspoon pepper
1/4 cup brown sugar
1 tablespoon butter
1/4 cup bread crumbs

Oven 350°   4 to 6 Servings

Sautée onion in butter in a large cast iron skillet. Add tomatoes, salt, pepper and brown sugar. Boil hard and stir often, breaking up tomatoes, until mixture thickens to desired consistency. Place in a buttered baking dish.

Melt butter in small frying pan; toss bread crumbs in butter. Sprinkle over tomatoes. Bake 20 minutes.

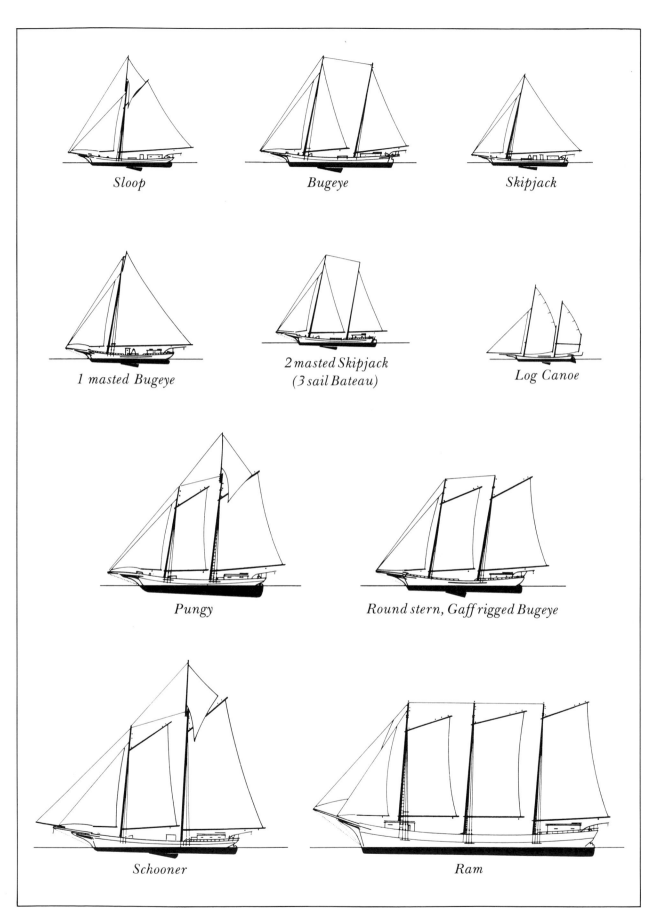

Sloop

Bugeye

Skipjack

1 masted Bugeye

2 masted Skipjack
(3 sail Bateau)

Log Canoe

Pungy

Round stern, Gaff rigged Bugeye

Schooner

Ram

BOATBUILDING ON THE BAY

Our earliest knowledge of boats in the area begins with the Indians, who used the dugout log canoe for inshore travel and fishing. Lacking tools, they used fire to fell the trees and burn the interiors of the logs, scraping out the charcoal and shaping the hull with shells. The first settlers adapted the log canoe to their uses, and with the benefit of more refined tools such as axes and adzes, improved the craft over the years.

With abundant forests so near the water, Talbot County led the newly-settled Maryland colony in boatbuilding, with the greatest concentration of yards in St. Michaels. At the close of the 1600s, however, better situated areas such as Baltimore, Norfolk and Annapolis had attracted most of the ocean-going vessel construction, leaving local yards to build the sloops, schooners, and small boats.

By the time of the Revolutionary War, boats were being designed more for speed than for cargo capacity. These were known as "clipper schooners" and reached the peak of their popularity during the War of 1812. Although known as "Baltimore Clippers," so many of them were built in St. Michaels yards they might just as well have been called "St. Michaels Clippers."

Boats were a necessity for local residents, who used them for both business and pleasure. In addition to sloops and schooners, the yards turned out shallops, bateaux, wherries, pirogues, and skiffs for Bay use, along with longboats, yawl boats, pinnaces, dories, and luggers for the ocean-going vessels built across the Bay.

The Indians' log canoe, after 250 years of evolution, became a sailing vessel by combining multiple logs into a "chunk." With the addition of sails and a centerboard, it was popular for tonging oysters. The ultimate log canoe was the bugeye, used for dredging oysters. A prime ex-

Ricky

MAST GLOP
Chesapeake Bay Maritime Museum

The Boat Shop's Paint Shed Recipe for Traditional Mast Coating—Chesapeake Bay Work Boats

3 parts varnish
2 parts boiled linseed oil
1 part turpentine

In a large container combine all ingredients; mix well; brush evenly on surface.

ample of the type, the *Edna E. Lockwood*, is displayed at the Museum. With the advent of engines, the log canoes faded from use and today are pleasure racing craft.

The sailing pungy was used for cargo hauling and has tall raked masts. Launched in 1986, the *Lady Maryland* is a replica of an 1800's pungy schooner which sails the Bay today as a floating classroom for children.

Skipjacks, appearing at the end of the century, replaced the bugeyes as dredgers of choice, since they were cheaper to build and maintain. In the early 1900s there were thousands of sailing dredgers, but by 1988 only 18 dredging licenses were issued. Tilghman Island harbors a majority of those still working. A fine skipjack example, the *Rosie Parks*, is a floating display at the Museum.

Schooners Drying Sails
Kirby & Sons Boatyard, St. Michaels, circa 1908; three schooners and a bugeye.

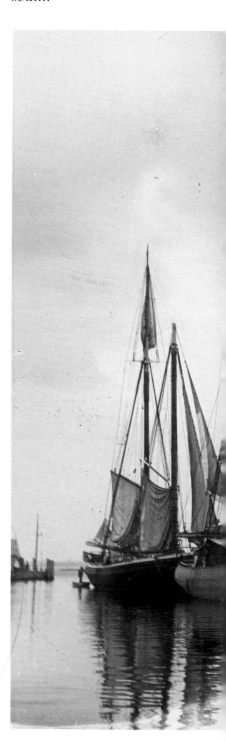

LILLY MAE'S SPECIAL POUND CAKE

In the early years of colonization, pound cake was a favorite dessert and various versions were published in many old cookbooks. The donor of this recipe believes this one may be traceable to the *Mayflower* by way of a family member named Peter Brown, who was a carpenter on that ship.

Preparation time for this delicious, no-fail cake is 15 minutes.

3 cups all purpose flour
1 teaspoon baking powder
1/4 teaspoon salt
1/2 pound butter
1/4 cup solid vegetable shortening
3 cups sugar
6 eggs
1 cup milk
1 teaspoon vanilla extract
1/2 teaspoon lemon extract

Oven 325°

Grease and flour an angel food cake pan; set aside. Sift dry ingredients; set aside.

In large mixing bowl cream butter, shortening, and sugar; add eggs one at a time, beating well after each addition. Add sifted dry ingredients to butter mixture alternately with milk, beating until smooth. Add flavorings; pour into cake pan.

Bake 1-1/2 hours.

ENTERPRIZE

Enterprize, *shown in an engraving based on a contemporary painting by Michel Corné, engages the British brig* Boxer *off the coast of Maine.*

In 1799, the U.S. Navy ordered two fast schooners for action in the quasi-war against France. One of the hulls was built in Henry Spencer's shipyard in St. Michaels, and Navy records indicate that she was probably the one christened *Enterprize* (sic).

According to naval historian Howard Chapelle, many fast Eastern-Shore-built schooners were sold to the French after the American Revolution. When the quasi-war broke out, our Navy had no boats fast enough to engage the French, so the Navy chose an Eastern Shore yard to build a competitive vessel.

With the sharp bow and sweeping lines of a Baltimore clipper, *Enterprize* was framed with oak and planked with white pine, measuring 84 feet on deck. Originally rigged as a schooner with 12 six-pound guns and crew of 76 officers and men, she was fast in light weather and sailed well to windward. Her cost was $16,240, including the outfitting work done in Baltimore.

Enterprize captured seven French vessels in the West Indies and was then ordered to the Mediterranean to join the war against the Barbary pirates. Sometime between 1809 and 1811, *Enterprize* was re-rigged as a brig and her armaments and crew were increased. The addition of more square sails and extra weight so handicapped most of the Navy's re-rigged schooners that they were captured by the British early in the war of 1812, but *Enterprize* survived and earned the nickname "Lucky *Enterprize*."

After the peace treaty with Great Britain, she returned to the Mediterranean to fight Algerian pirates who had been harassing U.S. shipping, and later fought pirates in the Caribbean. In August, 1823, she ran aground and was wrecked off Little Curacao.

Edna E. Lockwood

The Story of a Bugeye

Edna is the centerpiece of the Museum's floating exhibits, a rare example of a design that flourished for only a few decades. She is a double-ended 9-log bugeye ketch with a patent stern. She measures 54 feet on deck, 55 feet at the waterline, 17 feet in beam, and 2.7 feet in draft with centerboard up. Acquired in 1973 and relaunched after extensive refit in 1979, she celebrates her centennial in 1989.

On October 5, 1889 *Edna* was officially licensed "to carry on the coasting trade" with Daniel W. Haddaway, owner, and Oakly Cummings, master. Mr. Haddaway also signed the Master Carpenter's Certificate, lending weight to the assertion that he was the builder. Countering this evidence, John B. Harrison, when asked whether he built the *Lockwood*, answered in the affirmative. Harrison, too, was a noted bugeye builder, while Daniel Haddaway is not credited with building any other bugeyes, although he probably assisted in the *Lockwood's* construction.

The origin of her name is as yet unknown. The mystery of the lineage of *Edna Lockwood* has not been solved to this day, although many assertions have been made over the years. Even today, the search for *Edna's* namesake is continuing.

The bugeye traces its lineage to the brogan which, in turn, was a stage in the development of the early single log canoes prevalent on the Chesapeake. When oyster dredging was resumed after the Civil War, it was restricted to sailing vessels only. None of the then-existing types was suitable to the task; schooners' sides were too high, and pungies drew too much water. The bugeye's patent stern increased the afterdeck by adding a square, flat area above the narrow after-sections of the hull. The first bugeye met the water in about 1867 and the last log-built one in 1895, when the supply of suitable trees had dwindled.

The origin of the name, "bugeye," has many theories, none provable. *The Baltimore Sun* on December 31, 1901 printed a brief piece describing Captain Clement Sterling of Somerset who, on little more than a whim, decided to add two logs and a deck to his three-log canoe. When he sailed in this strange rig for Baltimore, he answered repeated hails of "What the deuce is that?!" with, "Why, it's a bug's eye!" And the name stuck.

Edna E. Lockwood
Though the life expectancy of a work boat on the Chesapeake at the time of her construction was about 20 years, the Edna E. Lockwood *has seen five times that many years, celebrating 100 years in 1989.* Edna *is believed to be the only log bugeye still sailing.*

A CHESAPEAKE CRABBER'S DICTIONARY

Buckram—crab whose shell has not quite hardened

Buster—molting crab whose shell has split

Channeler—large, mature male crab (*also* **jimmie**)

Chicken necker—weekend or amateur crabber

Dead men's fingers—crab's gills or lungs (*also* **devil's fingers**)

Doubler—male crab carrying female for mating (*also* **buck and rider**)

Hard crab—mature crab between molts

Keeper—legal-size catch

Molt—shedding of hard shell

Number ones—largest crabs

Paper shell—crab whose shell is beginning to harden after molting

Peeler—crab about to shed

Pickle—brine used to preserve bait

Pot—trap used mostly by deep water crabbers

Sally—immature female

Scrape—dredge

She crab—mature female crab (*also* **sook** *and* **sooky**)

Slabs—very large soft crabs (*also* **whales**)

Snoods—lines tied to a trotline from which bait is hung

'S not—'s not a hard crab and 's not a peeler

Soft shell crab—crab that has just molted whose shell has not hardened

Sponge crab—female carrying egg mass

Stills—dead crabs

Trotline—long baited line that rests on river and creek bottoms which is buoyed and anchored at each end

The Chesapeake Bay has provided more crabs for human consumption than any other body of water in the world. As *Callinectes sapidus*, a Latin term meaning "beautiful swimmer," the Chesapeake Bay blue crab reigns as undisputed king of Maryland's tidewater region.

The blue crab's nobility, however, ends in a somewhat untimely manner, given his rather tender age. Although some live three or more years, few crabs survive more than two. It takes almost that length of time to reach the adult size of four-plus inches. A crab will shed its shell, or molt, five or six times in the course of its lifetime. In that short period of time the crab develops, depending on temperature and conditions.

Mating is a prolonged and tender process, occurring during the period from late spring to early summer, but can occur any time except the dead of winter. A "jimmie" (male) will cradle a mature "sook" (female) beneath him for at least two days during her final molting and receptive period. Mating occurs between the time the female sheds her former shell and a new one begins to harden, a period of just a few hours. After mating and until the female's new shell has hard-

In commercial crab houses, crabs are steamed in large cylindrical pots often at the rate of 1,200 pounds in 12 minutes. After cooling, they are loaded onto tables where they are picked and sorted by grade.

ened, the jimmie continues to protect her in the cradle-carrying position. Then, the female heads for the lower Bay, storing the sperm until spring when she releases her eggs. Of two million or so eggs, perhaps only two will survive to become adults.

Highly sensitive to changes in the environment, the crab migrates south as water temperatures fall, searching out the depths where warmer waters prevail. In early winter, he buries himself in mud until spring, when he heads north to enter creeks, coves, and harbors.

A Maryland adage exclaims, "Don't be a crab, or a waterman'll get ya!" In a variety of less than dignified ways, the crab is pulled, kicking and fighting, from the watery kingdom he rules. Then, it's into the steaming kettle, where he becomes the major ingredient in one of Maryland's most popular meals—the crab feast—a pile of highly seasoned steamed crabs and a pitcher of cold beer.

CRAB MEAT TOSSED ON TOAST

A simple Eastern Shore favorite. Easy to prepare and pure in rich crab flavor. Sliced tomatoes and corn-on-the-cob complete the meal.

1/2 cup butter
2 teaspoons cider vinegar or sherry
1 pound lump crab meat
1 teaspoon flour
1/2 cup milk *or* half and half
Salt, pepper, and seafood seasoning to taste
4 slices bread, toasted

OPTIONAL TOPPINGS:
Crumbled bacon
julienne pieces of ham
grated cheese
minced scallions

4 Servings

In a large skillet melt butter; add vinegar or sherry and crab meat. Sautée until well combined and heated through. Sprinkle flour over all and, stirring constantly, add milk or half and half until thickened. Add seasonings to taste. Serve over toast; optional toppings as desired.

THE INCOMPARABLE OYSTER

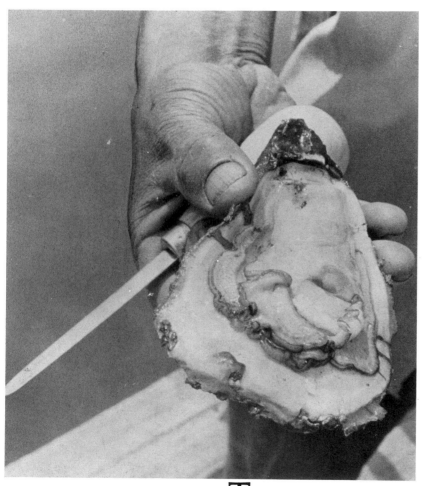

essentially built on land-fills of oyster shell, including the village of St. Michaels and some of its neighbors.

While oysters have always been sought primarily for food, the shells have been widely used for paving and also as aggregate in concrete and mortar. Ground oyster shell reinforces the mortar of the Bruton Parish Church in Williamsburg, Virginia.

Unfortunately, over-exploitation and urbanization have destroyed or restricted much of the oyster's habitat, including significant portions of the Chesapeake Bay. After the oyster resources of New England and New York were seriously depleted in the 19th century, intensive and largely uncontrolled oyster harvesting began in Chesapeake Bay, accompanied by animosity and even armed conflict between northern intruders and Maryland and Virginia watermen. In an attempt to regulate the industry and quell the violence, the State of Maryland established an "Oyster Navy" shortly after the Civil War—the progenitor of the present Natural Resources Police. Traces of animosity still persist today between some Maryland and Virginia watermen.

Recognizing the vulnera-

To say that life on the Eastern Shore of Maryland, Virginia, and many other tidewater communities has been historically based on the American oyster is more than just a figure of speech. From New England to the Gulf of Mexico, many small communities along the shoreline are

bility of their oyster resources, all the shoreline states now closely regulate shellfish harvesting, attempting to ensure a reasonably abundant supply. Federal agencies set public health standards for shellfish shipped between states.

While biologists have identified more than 100 species world-wide, only two edible species are native to the U.S., the American oyster of the East coast and the Olympia oyster of the West Coast. Typically residents of bays, sounds, and estuaries, the oyster's swimming larvae attach to hard surfaces such as rocks, pilings, and mollusk shells, where they eventually become baby oysters or spat.

Only a small fraction of oyster progeny survive, since they are prey for everything from newborn fish to jellyfish. Oystering is forbidden in the Chesapeake Bay and other East Coast waters during the summer to permit the brood stocks to spawn.

Reaching sexual maturity after one year, most oysters are male. During their lifetime they may switch sex to female and then, with advancing age, back to male.

No marine invertebrate has been more eagerly sought or avidly eaten than the oys-

SPRY CHEEZUM'S ORIGINAL OYSTER STEW

1 pint shucked oysters with their liquor
   Note: **If using personally shucked oysters, there will be plenty of natural liquid; if using purchased oysters, add about 1/2 teaspoon salt.**
1 pint half and half
Butter
Worcestershire sauce
Old Bay seasoning

In saucepan heat oysters with their liquor until the edges curl. In another saucepan heat half and half over medium heat until hot. Place oysters in individual serving bowls; pour heated half and half over oysters. Melt a pat of butter on each serving; add a dash of worcestershire sauce and Old Bay seasoning to taste.

ter. Records of oyster consumption date back to antiquity and they were even among the delicacies favored by Roman nobility at their infamous feasts.

THE OYSTER
The oyster's a confusing suitor:
It's masc., and fem., and even neuter.
At times it wonders, may what come,
Am I husband, wife, or chum.

Verses From 1929 On, by Ogden Nash
Copyright by Ogden Nash
By permission of Little, Brown and Company

CLAM FRITTERS

The French have beignets; the rest of the world has fritters. But the Eastern Shore has its own unique version which can only be described as saucer-sized "incredible edibles." The batter is not quite as thick as a dumpling-like fritter and not as thin as pancake batter. The result is a flatter, crisper, more delectable seafood fritter. Serve with pepper relish.

1 to 1-1/2 pints chopped clams *or* shucked oysters
1-3/4 cups flour
1 tablespoon baking powder
Salt and pepper to taste
2 teaspoons Old Bay seasoning
1 cup milk
2 eggs, beaten
1 tablespoon melted butter
Dash Tabasco
Cooking oil or solid vegetable shortening

Reserve liquor from seafood. Sift dry ingredients into a large mixing bowl. In a small bowl combine milk, eggs, butter, Tabasco, and clams or oysters; add to dry ingredients, mixing well. Batter should be of a pourable consistency. If too thick, add clam or oyster liquor or milk to thin.

In a large frying pan, pour cooking oil to a depth of 2 inches; heat. Pour about 1/2 cup batter (per fritter) into hot oil; fry about 2-1/2 minutes on each side until very brown and crisp on edges. Drain on paper towels.

Soft-shell clams (maninose—"manos") have been difficult to harvest commercially on the Chesapeake Bay because the tide range is not great enough to expose the sand bars where the clams live.

Prior to the 1950s clams were traditionally harvested with a clam rake in shallow water or by churning up the bottom with a boat's propeller and netting the clams. In the 1950s the hydraulic dredge and conveyer was developed experimentally in Eastern Bay and the Miles River. A dredging rig is equipped with a hose which digs a trench in river bottoms 30 inches wide and 18 inches deep. Clams are forced onto a conveyer belt which brings them to the boat.

Today clamming is becoming an important area industry, with an estimated annual potential harvest of 500,000 bushels.

TERRAPIN *Epicure's Delight* •

They're the main ingredient in that most patrician of American dishes—terrapin. To the devotee, that's it— "terrapin"—not "terrapin soup" or "terrapin stew." John Dorsey, former restaurant critic for the *Baltimore Sun*, describes it as "slightly sweet, deliciously rich and at the same time subtle, but otherwise indescribable." No wonder it was once the ultimate dining experience for such famous men as General Winfield Scott, the Marquis de Lafayette, and Florenz Ziegfield.

The waters and swamps of the Chesapeake have always abounded with terrapin. In summer and fall hunters would dig long shallow

TERRAPIN PREPARATION

Get a specimen 7 to 8 inches long. It's sure to be a cow and will be carrying a bevy of eggs. Add a pound of baking soda to a gallon of water and bring to a high boil. If your catch sticks her head out, chop it off. If she hides in her shell, press on her back with your palm and she'll stick her neck out to see what's going on.

Proceed with the execution. Dip her body in the boiling water three times for about 30 seconds each. Using a piece of rough cloth, rub the skin off all protruding parts except the tail, which you'll soon discard. Slit between the shells with a stout knife and scrape out all the loose entrails together with the heart, lungs, and tail. Remove the eggs, wash them off and put them aside. The gall is a marble-sized dark green sac attached to the liver. Be very careful not to break it as you slice it away or you'll have to find another terrapin. Pull the nails out and separate the liver and other meaty portions from the shell. Cover these with water and dump in the eggs. Boil the lot for about an hour and a half. Strain the stock and save. Separate the meat from the bones and put aside with the eggs. Put the bones back in the stock and simmer for two hours. Discard the bones and pour the stock over the meat. Remove the eggs from their membrane-like shells, chop them up and add to the mixture. Season with salt, pepper, 4 ounces of a good dry sherry, a half tablespoon of prepared mustard, and an ounce of chicken bouillon. Make a roux with a stick of butter and a cup of flour. Add the roux and a tablespoon of gravy browning to the batch and simmer for 30 minutes. Finally, add a pinch of rosemary and more salt and pepper to taste. Serve from a tureen or chafing dish with Maryland beaten biscuits and side dishes of your choice. And don't forget the wine— sherry, madeira or champagne.

ditches across the tidal marshes at low tide. When the tide came in, lazy terrapin found the bottom already prepared and burrowed in for winter hibernation. As the tides brought in a layer of mud and a new catch, the hunter probed his ditch with a pitchfork and dug out the prize.

As terrapin came into vogue in the second half of the 1800s, the price began at $2 a dozen, but by 1900 it had increased to $70 a dozen. By the end of World War I, demand, particularly on the part of Baltimore epicureans and their visitors, brought about the need for conservation measures. Open season was only from November 1 until March 31, and it was unlawful to disturb nests or take any eggs that had been laid. Talbot County even had a law that only county residents could take terrapin from its waters.

Then came prohibition. Since sherry wine is used in terrapin preparation and wine is a necessary accompaniment to its consumption, demand for terrapin fell along with availability of liquor. Sadly, due to the period of time when it was rarely served and the advent of the fast food era, the dish has never regained its popularity. Today, open season is year round, but now a terrapin for the pot must be at least six inches long and the same list of restrictions still applies.

Preparing terrapin in the Bay Hundred district might be as extinct an art as barbecuing dinosaur were it not for a few true natives and two chefs at local restaurants who are thinking of putting it on their menus.

WATERFOWLING·
AND MARKET GUNNING

"The life of man is divided into two seasons: Geese is here. Geese ain't here."

–Lafe Turlock, from *Chesapeake*

Hunting waterfowl in the Chesapeake Bay area predates colonization. The Indians used bows, arrows, nets, and decoys made of mud and grasses (later called "tumps" by watermen).

The colonists stalked the birds with their "fowling pieces," flintlocks up to six feet long, shooting birds while they were feeding or at rest. Wing shooting was rare until the early 1800s. Night hunting by firelight was stopped by the powerful landholders around 1700 for the reason that it frightened the waterfowl away at night, depriving the more numerous daytime hunters of shooting opportunities.

Until the mid-1800s, hunting was limited to food for the table of family and neighbors. Soon, however, restaurants, hotels, and clubs began to demand not only Bay seafood for their menus, but waterfowl as well.

This demand gave rise to another source of income for many watermen, that of market gunning. Waterfowl hunting became so uncontrolled that soon laws were enacted to halt the indiscriminate killing. Most significant was the federal Migratory Bird Treaty Act of 1918 and the establishment of the National Fish and Wildlife Service. Initially, the law had the effect of turning legitimate market hunters into outlaws, as they continued to use their accustomed hunting methods which had now become illegal.

These included the big punt guns, some nine feet long, that could shoot 75 birds with one shot, and the pipe and battery guns, which were a series of muzzles, set in a fanlike design, which fired simultaneously. Some of this shooting was done at night using a bow light. Other illegal forms were use of the sinkbox, baiting of any kind, and trapping.

The one constant throughout the history of waterfowling, from the flintlock to the automatic shotgun, has been the use of decoys—whether a "tump," carved piece of wood, silhouette, fabric, or plastic model. Only tollers

(Overleaf) Hunters in the blind.

63

"I can eat it roasted, or chopped with onions and peppers, or sliced thin with mushrooms," Lafe Turlock was telling the men at the store. "You can keep the other months of the year, just give me November with a fat goose comin' onto the stove three times a week."

—From *Chesapeake*

HUNTER'S GLOSSARY

Bushwack Boat—ferry for gunners, floating blind; *also* **run boat**
Can—canvasback duck
Canada—Canada goose
Corning—baiting with corn; "A duck ain't worth a damn 'lessen it's been corn fed."
Flats, The—confluence of the Susquehanna, Northeast, Elk, and Bohemia Rivers
Hangs—gun misfires
John goose—decoy used to mark a hunter's spot
Knot—tight formation of birds
Lay boats—support boats, floating quarters
Loom up—waterfowl swimming towards a night hunter's light (illegal)
Low in—birds passing over decoys
Pitch in—landing
Plogger—skilled marsh hunter
Proggin'—poking around marshy creeks and pot holes, catching whatever is available
Pointup—lead bird sets direction for formation
Pull down—take aim and fire
Raft—cluster of waterfowl
Right up a stovepipe—rapid vertical climb
Rounding out—making a turn
Spook—to scare or startle
Stool—rig of decoys
Stringer—a trail of bait
Stump jumper—an occasional hunter
Sure as gun iron—absolute, certain
Tail to—bird swinging into the wind
Water pheasant—mergansers, *also* **shelldrakes, saw bills, water witches**

(live decoys that could lure in wild birds) have been banned.

Insofar as bird types are concerned, the waterfowl population has changed over the years. Prior to the 1930s ducks were dominant while geese were uncommon. Today, the Canada goose predominates and is the prime target of the waterfowl hunter.

Hunting has become purely a sport. Gone are the days when a party could shoot 75 birds in 15 minutes, 200 in a day. Now the bag limit is determined by a point system. Most shooting is done

from blinds, although body booting (a body boot is a one-piece rubber suit complete with boots which comes up under the arms) has its advocates.

Migratory game laws are enforced by the National Fish and Wildlife Service and the Maryland Department of Natural Resources.

Decoy Carver's Workshop

From *The Frugal Housewife*, or *Complete Woman Cook*, 1802:

"To Roast A Turkey, Goose, Duck, Fowl, etc."
When you roast a turkey, goose, fowl, or chicken, lay them down to a good fire. Singe them clean with white paper, baste them with butter, and dust on some flour. As to time, a large turkey will take an hour and twenty minutes; a middling one a full hour; a full-grown goose, if young, an hour; a large fowl, three-quarters of an hour; a middling one half an hour, and a small chicken, twenty minutes, but this depends entirely on the goodness of your fire.

When your fowls are thoroughly plump, and the smoke draws from the breast to the fire, you may be sure that they are very done. Then baste them with butter; dust on a very little flour, and as soon as they have a good froth, serve them up.

Geese and ducks are commonly seasoned with onions, sage, and a little pepper and salt.

CHESAPEAKE BAY HUNTING DOGS

The hunting of waterfowl is an important part of life on the Bay today just as it was for the Indians who first hunted ducks, geese, and other wild fowl. Prior to the development of the shotgun, when the primary hunting weapon was the bow and arrow, there was no need for a dog to retrieve fallen game. Retrievers owe their existence to the shotgun, since it is the function of a well-trained hunting dog to retrieve on command from land or water.

The three principal breeds of hunting dog which have proven most popular on the Bay are the Golden Retriever, the Labrador Retriever, and the Chesapeake Bay Retriever, which is considered to be the only native-bred hunting dog.

The Chesapeake is a big, burly dog with an independent, even stubborn, streak. It was developed by market gunners as a heavy-duty water retriever, and in those times could retrieve over 100 ducks in a day from icy water.

All Chesapeakes are descended from Sailor and Canton, Newfoundland puppies saved from a shipwreck in 1807. Whether by accident or design, they bred with the watermen's dogs, and contin-

ued cross-breeding resulted in the developed dog by 1885. The AKC recognized the breed in 1887.

A dog of great endurance, the Chesapeake will seem to swim and retrieve all day if asked. With their double-oily coat, they seem practically immune to icy water. Males average 70 to 80 pounds; females weigh 60 to 70 pounds. Because the Chesapeake is a big dog, it is happier where it has a bit of room. It is extremely protective of its home and family.

The Labrador Retriever is by far the most popular of all retrievers, according to numbers registered. It is a fast and stylish performer, a dependable retriever both on land and in the water. The Lab's disposition is noted for its gentleness, and it makes a good house dog. However, it has a reputation as a hobo, and likes to wander from time to time.

An attractive dog with a mild disposition, the Golden Retriever has a difficult time competing in field trials against the Labrador because it doesn't have the same drive and dash. The Golden's best work is done in small marshes and prairie potholes. It makes a fine, loyal family pet and is very good with children.

The Museum's iron dog, a Newfoundland, was cast in the 1850's by a Baltimore iron maker in memory of "Sailor" and "Canton," from whom the Chesapeake Bay Retriever descends.

RETRIEVER TREATS

Not just for retrievers, these biscuits are relished by all kinds of dogs—white ones, brown ones, big ones, little ones, and even classic Chesapeake Bay Retrievers "Jukes" and "Jenna" above—and the garlic helps keep fleas at bay. (*Note*: These aren't bad as people treats.)

2 cups whole wheat flour
1/2 cup cornmeal
1 clove garlic, minced
1/2 cup finely grated
   cheddar cheese

1 egg
1/4 cup cooking oil
1 beef bouillon cube dis-
   solved in 1/2 cup water

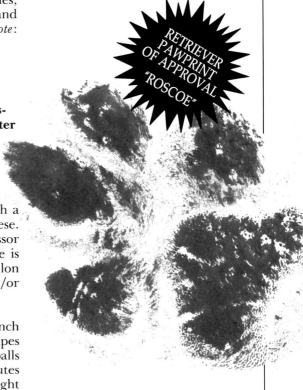

RETRIEVER PAWPRINT OF APPROVAL "ROSCOE"

Oven 350°

In the bowl of a food processor (or in a large bowl with a pastry blender), combine flour, cornmeal, garlic, and cheese. In small bowl, whisk egg and oil. With the food processor running, add egg/oil mixture and process until mixture is evenly crumbly. With processor still running, add bouillon until a ball forms. (If dough is too stiff, add more oil and/or cheese as necessary.)

Roll out dough on an ungreased surface to nearly 1/2-inch thick. Cut with a bone-shaped cutter or into tempting shapes such as cats, trees, mailmen, fire hydrants, or just plain balls or sticks. Place on greased baking sheets; bake 30 minutes and let cool completely on a wire rack. Store in an air-tight container.

MUSKRAT RAMBLINGS

Described as "marsh rabbit" and considered a delicacy on some area restaurant menus, muskrat found its way to these tables by chance. Farmers have always viewed the aquatic rodents as pests; however, in the days following the Civil War, a market was found for the pelts of these plump, furry animals.

At one time, St. Michaels had its own "fur house" on St. Mary's Square. Later, it was discovered that the strong, dark meat was delicious if properly prepared.

Preparation methods vary with individual preference, but generally involve stewing or baking. However muskrat is prepared, it is essential that

Ondatra zibethica

it be soaked in salt water (4 to 5 tablespoons salt in a large container) for 3 to 4 hours (to draw blood out and remove gamey flavor). After soaking, it should be rinsed thoroughly, then cut into pieces (hind quarter, front quarter, and middle section).

Referred to simply as "rats" by native residents, a muskrat menu is best accompanied by hot biscuits, scalloped potatoes, stewed tomatoes, and a fresh salad. "Rat" gravy may be made with the pan drippings, and the repast is pronounced a rare treat during the limited muskrat season of January and February. Generally, one muskrat will serve two persons, depending on how much you like 'em.

METHOD #1

1 muskrat, cut in pieces
1 apple, 1 potato and 1 onion, peeled and quartered
1/2 cup water
Seasonings to taste

Place muskrat pieces in heavy Dutch oven along with apple, potato and onion pieces. Add water; cover and cook over medium heat about one hour. (Length of cooking time depends upon age of the muskrat; meat should be fork tender.) Remove muskrat pieces to broiler pan; season to taste. Broil both sides until well browned.

METHOD #2

Muskrat, cut in pieces
Flour
Salt, pepper
Shortening
Water
Sliced onions
Quartered potatoes (optional)

Dredge muskrat pieces in flour; season to taste with salt and pepper; fry until browned on both sides. Place a rack in a large Dutch oven and add water up to rack. Cover with sliced onions and potatoes, if desired. (The onions and potatoes draw out gamey flavor and are discarded after cooking.) Cover Dutch oven and simmer until fork tender (about 45 minutes to one hour). Water level should be monitored occasionally. Discard onions and potatoes. Serve with rat gravy prepared from pan drippings.

METHOD #3

Muskrat, cut in pieces
Flour
Salt and pepper
Sage
Sliced onions
Bacon strips
1 cup water

Oven 350°

Dredge muskrat pieces in flour; place in shallow baking dish; season to taste with salt, pepper, and sage. Sprinkle sliced onions over all; lay bacon strips on top. Add water; cover with aluminum foil. Bake 1-1/4 hours; remove aluminum foil; bake another 15 minutes to brown.

STEAMBOATIN' AND BOARDING HOUSE DAYS

A Sentimental Journey

The Chesapeake's most romantic era commenced about 1813 with the appearance of the first sidewheeler, the *S.S. Chesapeake*, in Baltimore Harbor. The sound of her whistle brought families with brimming picnic baskets, school children celebrating graduation days, and couples out for an evening cruise.

On the great turn-of-the-century steamboats many a romance blossomed and engagements were made as couples danced to bands or strolled on deck in the moonlight. Gentlemen bought their favorite ladies 10-cent ginger ales in green, hexagonal-shaped bottles. Back then people of all ages reveled in the excitement of a steamboat trip.

For many years steamboats were the heart of transportation and commerce between Baltimore and the tidewater region. Eventually more than 250 steamers vied for passengers on the Bay. As competition grew, better services and accommodations became available, and the cuisine kept pace. While ham, chicken, beef, oysters, crab, and fish were regularly served, diamondback terrapin, canvasback duck, quail, wild goose, and rabbit found their way into the elegant dining salons. Inventive methods of food preparation evolved—vegetables were prepared using the engine's steam and a spit for roasting meats was ingeniously turned by gears connected to paddle shafts.

While passengers enjoyed themselves above, farm implements and merchandise were shipped to Eastern Shore points in cargo holds below. Fresh farm produce from the region's rich agricultural lands and seafood harvested from the bountiful Bay were delivered back to cities on the return trip.

By 1911 Baltimore was connected by steamboat to more than 200 Chesapeake Bay getaways and resorts. A favorite destination on these shores was Claiborne, six miles up the road from St. Michaels. Claiborne owed its existence to the Baltimore, Chesapeake and Atlantic Railroad Company which established the town as a terminus in 1886.

Some passengers continued by train through St. Michaels and on to Ocean City and other resorts. Vacationers who stayed found guest and boarding houses offering excellent food and entertainment in serene country surroundings only a short carriage ride away. In those days, oyster shell roads led to nooks and crannies in this land of innumerable coves, creeks, and inlets.

The railroad company listed some 27 guest accommodations in the area, including Claiborne, McDaniel, St. Michaels, and Royal Oak. Weary city-dwellers found rest, relaxation, and memorable repasts in those Eastern Shore summers of the past at places like Wades Point Farm, Maple Hall, and The Pasadena.

The demise of the great paddle wheelers began with the advent of cars and trucks whose speeds could not be matched by these boats which cruised at a leisurely 12 to 14 miles per hour. With the Depression came the bankruptcy of many steamboat lines, and a century of romance was to fade away forever.

RUM SAUCE AND ROMANCE ABOARD THE EMMA GILES

The *Emma Giles* was one of the most popular excursion boats running from the Light Street piers in Baltimore to Eastern Shore destinations. Peach cobbler laced with rum sauce was one of her dessert specialties, while the refreshment stand off the social deck offered big, juicy lemons mounted on peppermint sticks.

Initials carved all over the ship's guardrails testified to the power of love—and steamboats. Though she was retired in 1939 and scrapped in 1959, an Annual Emma Giles Dinner has commemorated the big, graceful paddlewheeler for more than 10 years. The only steamboat with a fan club, its members meet yearly to swap *Emma Giles* stories.

WADES POINT FARM

McDaniel, Maryland

In 1895 the Wades Point Farm opened its door to paying guests, many of whom returned year after year to enjoy the hospitality and cuisine for which the guest house was famous. Meals were served family style to an average of 50 guests a day. Specialties of the house included home-cured hams, fried chicken, and a crab soup which had an ingredient no one could quite put his finger on. Although often asked what it was, the cook would not divulge the secret. Then one day while observing the process carefully, Mrs. Kemp watched the cook throw in a pinch of sugar. That was it!

Hearty breakfasts offered the usual fare, but fried tomatoes and chipped beef were not uncommon. Midday dinner was the main meal of the day and always consisted of soup, two meats, at

Thomas Kemp, noted area shipbuilder, bought the property in 1813 shortly after 1,800 British troops landed at Wades Point and severely damaged the previous house. Mr. Kemp built the present house and the property stayed in the family until 1984. The small structure atop the roof on the left was Mr. Kemp's "spy house" where he observed boats on Eastern Bay.

The cupola was known as "Lovers' Retreat"—seats around its interior made it a popular rendezvous point for couples in love who marked the spot by carving initials in the wall.

Known as the Wades Point Inn today, it is one of the area's bed and breakfast inns.

MILDRED KEMP'S SECRET INGREDIENT CRAB SOUP

1 small onion, finely chopped
1 green bell pepper, chopped
5 medium tomatoes, peeled and chopped *or* 1 28-ounce can tomatoes, drained and chopped
1 teaspoon dry mustard
1 pound crab meat
Salt and pepper to taste
1 tablespoon butter or margarine
1 tablespoon flour
1/4 teaspoon worcestershire sauce
1/4 teaspoon sugar
2 cups milk
1 cup half and half

In a medium saucepan place onion, green pepper, and tomatoes. Make a paste with the dry mustard and water; add to vegetables. Add water to cover; simmer until vegetables are soft. Drain water; stir in crab meat, salt, and pepper; set aside.

In a large sauce pan over medium heat, melt butter; blend in flour. Add worcestershire sauce and sugar. Slowly add milk and half and half, stirring constantly. Stir in vegetable and crab mixture. Soup should be heated through but not boiled.

least three vegetables, plus home-baked breads and desserts. Oyster roasts were popular at Wades Point Farm and, over the years, cooks enjoyed preparing their own favorite dishes such as spoon bread, rice custard, apple betty, and lemon pie.

Drinking was forbidden in the main house, but guests could enjoy a social hour before or after dinner in "The Roost," a separate building with comfortable chairs. Dances and memorable parties with themes such as "Gone with the Wind" were held in the Pavilion.

THE PASADENA
Royal Oak, Maryland

The ad read, "For Sale, 'Rosedale,' 150 acres of waterfront farmland on the Eastern Shore of Maryland in Royal Oak." Seeking a warmer climate, the Harpers of Michigan moved in with their rapidly expanding family. After a second set of twins was born within 14 months, Mrs. Harper announced, "Let's take in boarders." In 1902 the Harper family first

opened their doors to paying guests.

Eventually, some members of the Harper family moved to Pasadena, California. Frederick Harper, however, stayed at Rosedale and vowed he would make it into a Pasadena. To this day, the establishment is known as "The Pasadena."

Typical of other boarding and guest houses, the menu featured fresh, local bounty. Almost without exception everything served was home-grown or raised. Country hams became a house specialty. It was Bill Harper's method for curing hams that earned him fame. One time he butchered a 700-pound hog and processed it into the usual 15 to 20 pound hams. It was one of these that captured a blue ribbon at an exhibition at the old Easton armory, but it was his gargantuan 50-pounder that took second place the same year.

Smokehouses were as necessary to rural life then as microwave ovens are today. With as many as 50 hams in process at a time, Mr. Harper had two secrets for curing: a layer of fat was allowed to remain on each ham so that the meat stayed moist, and fresh fires were built daily from the stumps of old apple trees for smoke that would impart a special flavor. The recipe included rubbing into each ham a mixture of either honey (harvested from the 25 to 30 hives on the property), or molasses, along with salt, plenty of pepper, and brown sugar.

Guests enjoyed watersports and entertainments typical of the times as well as watermelon feeds on the dock, crab feasts, masked balls, talent shows, plays, and bands every night of the week except Sunday. A claim to fame unique to The Pasadena was the filming of "The First Kiss" in 1928 starring Fay Wray and Gary Cooper. During the six weeks of filming, 60 crew members and the stars of the show were treated as regular guests. Chances are they enjoyed The Pasadena's Crab Imperial which was much in demand by those who stayed there.

Today The Pasadena still operates as an inn and conference center offering home cooked meals in the old plantation house.

THE PASADENA'S CRAB IMPERIAL

Over the years The Pasadena's specialties included home cured hams, Etta-the-cook's incredible souffles, lacy corn cakes, fluffy omelets, and their often requested Crab Imperial.

2 tablespoons butter
2 tablespoons flour
2 cups light cream
2 egg yolks
1/2 teaspoon salt
1 teaspoon dry mustard
1 teaspoon worcestershire sauce
Dash red pepper
1 pound crab meat
Cracker or bread crumbs
Butter

Oven 350°   4 to 6 Servings

In a large saucepan melt butter; stirring constantly add flour and blend in cream; set aside. In a small bowl beat together egg yolks, salt, dry mustard, worcestershire sauce, and red pepper. Add to cream sauce. Place crab meat in a casserole and pour cream sauce over all. Sprinkle crumbs on top; dot with butter. Bake about 15 minutes.

Maple Hall
Claiborne, Maryland

The Misses Sarah and Mary Carolyn Cockey, St. Michaels residents whose family ran Maple Hall for generations, recall:

"When the dinner bell rang at Maple Hall, 50 guests or more sat down to tables set with fresh-cut flowers and wonderful Eastern Shore meals; good, plain country cooking, simply prepared. Meals were served at regular hours: breakfast at 8, mid-day dinner at 1 and supper at 6.

Anna's Shortcake

The batter of this generations-old Delmarva receipt is so buttery-rich and flavorful straight from the bowl, it's almost a shame to bake it. *Anna's Shortcake*, topped with rum-laced fresh fruit and served with whipped cream, could rival apple pie as *the* classic American dessert.

1/2 cup butter or margarine (at room temperature)
1-1/3 cups sugar
2 eggs
1 teaspoon vanilla *or* rum extract
2 cups self-rising flour
1-1/3 cups buttermilk
3 cups fresh strawberries, raspberries, or peaches
2 tablespoons dark rum
1/2 cup sugar
2 cups heavy cream, whipped

Oven 400°

Grease and flour a No. 7 cast iron skillet (or a deep 10-inch pie pan); set aside. In a large bowl, cream butter and sugar; beat in eggs, vanilla or rum extract, flour, and buttermilk; beat until smooth. Bake 30 minutes or until a knife inserted in center comes out clean. In a large bowl mix fruit with rum and sugar; spoon over split slices of cake; top with whipped cream.

Many guests loved to fish so there was always plenty of fresh seafood on the menu. A large vegetable garden produced plentifully and preserves were made from the damson, peach, fig, pear, and apple trees on the farm. White Queen Anne cherries were preserved and served over sweet potato pie. Cows provided milk and cream, and pigs, sheep, chickens, goats, turkeys, and guinea hens were part of the farm stock. We particularly enjoyed helping with the sausage making. Muskrat was served at our tables and if you didn't know what it was, it tasted rather like chicken. Mock terrapin (calf's liver) was also served.

Fresh breads and other baked goods were prepared using the old wood-burning cookstove. 'Pocketbook rolls' were made by rolling out raised dough, cutting it with a round cookie cutter, and putting a pool of melted butter on the dough. Then they were folded over, making a 'pocket.' A wonderful yellow cake with caramel icing had black walnuts from the trees on the farm; one of the cooks was known for the strawberry shortcake she made.

On the Fourth of July and for Sunday dinner there was always fried chicken. Birthdays were special occasions at Maple Hall and one of our aunts had an especially delicate hand at decorating the cakes. Home-made vanilla, peach, or strawberry ice cream appeared on lots of occasions.

There were two stores in Claiborne for things we didn't grow or raise ourselves and a wagon would deliver blocks of ice from the ice house in St. Michaels.

People always seemed to enjoy themselves at Maple Hall. There was swimming in Tilghman's Creek and good water depth for boats. We had tennis courts and a golf course; some people played baseball, croquet, or quoits on the lawn."

Today Maple Hall is a private residence. For those who stayed there during the height of the steamboat era, a lifetime of memories remain.

"THE FIRST KISS"

Gary Cooper and Fay Wray, above, aboard an oyster schooner in a scene from the 1928 Hollywood movie, "The First Kiss."

A postcard depicts Paramount producing "The First Kiss," St. Michaels, Maryland

Paramount Producing "The First Kiss", St. Michaels, Md.

"The First Kiss", Gary Cooper's first starring movie, was filmed in St. Michaels, Royal Oak, and Easton. It was adapted from a *Saturday Evening Post* story, "Four Brothers," written by Tristam Tupper while Mr. Tupper was at Maple Hall in Claiborne.

In 1928 Hollywood sent a cast and crew to the St. Michaels area to make the movie starring, according to the Easton newspaper, "Gary Gopper and Fay Wray." It was one of the last big budget silent movies, costing $200,000. The St. Michaels oyster fleet was put under contract by the studio, with several watermen having bit parts. About 200 residents of the county were hired as extras, but when the picture premiered at the Avalon Theater in Easton, their scenes had been redone by Hollywood extras.

The story line told of an oyster dredger who turned to piracy to put his brothers through college. He also was in love with a wealthy young lady, who first rebuffed him but later returned his love. Some critics called the plot "impossible and overdone." The general consensus at the time was that it was "one of the worst films ever made." No prints of the picture have apparently survived.

THE ORIGINAL·
SHOWBOAT "The Opry Barge"

Live entertainment was available during the summer to ports on the Bay from 1914 to 1941. It came with the arrival of "The James Adams Floating Theatre," a 128-foot, three-decked barge drawing only 14 inches of water. There were living quarters for 32, plus 10 dressing rooms. Not having power, it depended on its tugs *Elk* and *Trouper* which, after docking the barge, would cruise the creeks and coves advertising the presence of the theater, sometimes called "The Opry Barge" by the patrons.

The repertoire included such melodramas as *The Girl of the Golden West, East Lynne, The Big Shot, Kentucky Colonels,* and *St. Elmo.* The most popular was *Ten Nights in a Barroom.* Adams' sister, Beulah, was the star for many years, billed as the "Mary Pickford of the Chesapeake." She kept up the illusion into her 50s with makeup and curly-haired wigs.

Admission was 25¢ and 50¢, with an additional 10¢ and 15¢ for the variety concert that followed, which was billed as "The Whiz Bang Revue."

An entrance through the orchestra pit led to the dining room and galley. Here meals

A former player recalls:
"We ate twice a day, at 10:30 a.m. and 4:30 p.m. The food was good and there was lots of it. For breakfast we would have hot biscuits, eggs, corned beef hash, bacon, herring roe, scrapple, milk and coffee. For dinner there were at least six vegetables and a stew, or chicken, roast, ham or fish. And it was on the showboat that I first encountered that Southern delicacy (?) fatback and collards."

CREAMED SPINACH

For five generations this colorful side dish has traditionally appeared on the Thanksgiving sideboard of the Tucker-Hickey family. Take a bow when serving it whether prepared with spinach or other greens such as collards, kale, mustard, or turnip.

2 pounds fresh spinach, washed and stemmed *or* **2
   10-ounce packages frozen chopped spinach**
1 cup water
8 strips bacon
1 medium-large onion, chopped
1/2 cup flour
Salt and pepper to taste
Dash nutmeg

In large saucepan, cook spinach in water until fork tender; reserving liquid, drain spinach; chop (if using fresh greens) and set aside. In a large skillet fry bacon until crisp; reserving pan drippings, drain bacon; crumble; set aside. Sauté onion in bacon drippings until translucent; add crumbled bacon.

Lower heat and, stirring constantly, add flour a little at a time to form a roux-like paste (mixture should form a ball). Stirring constantly, add liquid from spinach until a thick sauce results (add additional water, if necessary). Add spinach and seasonings; combine well; simmer 5 to 10 minutes.

for cast and crew were prepared by an excellent staff of cooks.

Another recollection is that of Rosa Teel who "bossed the baking of soda biscuits and frying of fish for ten years; assistant cooks prepared great platters of tomato salad for the supper table."

Between acts hawkers sold boxes of Crackerjacks. After the show players snacked on sandwiches, salads, and coffee served in the various dressing rooms.

In 1928 Edna Ferber was a guest aboard while she gathered material for "Show Boat." The popularity of the book and play prompted the owners to change the name to "The Original Floating Theatre."

Competition from motion pictures and limited docking facilities forced the new owners to abandon activity in 1941. It was destined to become a cargo barge but, before that conversion, it was fatefully destroyed by fire.

INSPIRATION BY THE BAY

EBENEZER COOKE

One of the first writers to give us a view of the Eastern Shore was Ebenezer Cooke. It is not clear whether Cooke was born in Maryland or in England, but he was familiar enough with Maryland to have derided her from every angle in his famous poem, "The Sot-weed Factor," written in 1708. The poem describes a tobacco merchant's hapless adventures on the Eastern Shore where he is swindled, harassed, and robbed by a variety of nefarious characters, outrageously exaggerated in burlesque descriptions.

Later versions include apologies, explanations, and deletions, for Cooke was to live and prosper in Maryland after his father's death. The timeless humor of "The Sotweed Factor" emerged over two and a half centuries later as the inspiration for John Barth's novel of the same title.

JOHN DICKINSON

John Dickinson, born in Talbot County in 1732, is known in contrast to Thomas Paine as the more conservative "penman of the Revolution." A true patriot, Dickinson wrote "A Song for American Freedom," published in 1768. His lyrics appealed to American birthrights of liberty and freedom from arbitrary rule and taxation by the Mother Country.

AMELIA BALL COPPUCK WELBY

The first Poet Laureate of Maryland was Amelia Ball Coppuck Welby, born in 1812. Edgar Allan Poe described Welby as one who "often surprises, and always delights by novel, rich, and accurate combination of the ancient musical expressions." Published at the age of 18, her verse is as romantically idealistic as Cooke's is sardonic. Welby's childhood home still stands today in St. Michaels, described pastorally in her poem below.

"Maryland Village in Moonlight"
. . . In distance away,
Rolled the Foam-crested waves of Chesapeake Bay,
While Bathed in the moonlight the village was seen
With the church in the distance, that stood on the green.
The soft-sloping meadows lay brightly unrolled,
With their mantles of verdure and blossoms of gold
And the earth in her beauty, forgetting to grieve,
Lay asleep in her bloom on the bosom of eve. . .

James A. Michener

If a single work is responsible for introducing the reading public to the Eastern Shore of Maryland, it is most certainly James A. Michener's novel, *Chesapeake*. His fascination for the Chesapeake began during his college years when he sailed the Bay with fellow students from Swarthmore College.

While working on *Chesapeake*, Michener's first-hand research took him out on oyster dredging and tonging boats, and occasioned many interviews with elders born and raised on the Shore. The novel, which chronicles four hundred years of Shore history, took three and one half years to research and write, much of it done at the Chesapeake Bay Maritime Museum.

Sophie Kerr

A different perspective of the Eastern Shore appears in stories by Sophie Kerr (Underwood), which describe details of everyday life around the turn of the century. It is the "land of milk and honey" where good manners and good food abound. An epicurean herself, Kerr's vivid descriptions of food in such stories as "Cupboard Lover" unfortunately do not include recipes. With over 20 published novels, Kerr's works include *Love At Large* and *The Sound of Petticoats and Other Stories of the Eastern Shore*.

Gilbert Byron

A local favorite, Gilbert Byron is noted for his poetry, his fiction, and vivid regional descriptions. Byron was born in Chestertown in 1903 and his love for the Eastern Shore is apparent in his frequent use of autobiographical material, his characters' colloquial voices, and their steadfast pride in the waterman's way of life.

In his novel, *The Lord's Oysters*, Byron recounts the adventures of Noah, an Eastern Shore oyster "drudger" as he sails his schooner on the Bay in search of the big haul. His poem, "The Eastern Shoreman," distills the rugged independence of that unique breed, the Chesapeake waterman.

"I like my liquor and my freedom
straight
And this points out our mortal
danger.
Citizens are watching citizens
And taking money for it. Stranger,
Us Shoremen don't have much use
For inspectors and their scheme.
We've got nothing but abuse
For any public spying.
Those would make a nightmare
Of our dream."

John Simmons Barth

John Simmons Barth, a native of Cambridge, Maryland, is a major American writer whose novel, "The Sot-weed Factor", has recreated the life and times of Ebenezer Cooke. Written in similar form and style to Rabelais' *Gargantua & Pantagruel*, Barth rivals his predecessor in bawdy images and ribald adventures. It is an historical satire which easily carries you back in time and place, laughing all the way.

Waters Edwin Turpin and Margaret Stavely

Writers Waters Edwin Turpin and Margaret Stavely, contemporaries born in Talbot County, bring personal insights of Bay life and times to their work. Turpin's novels, *These Low Grounds*, *O Canaan*, and *The Rootless*, trace the inequities suffered throughout history by the Black men and women of the Eastern Shore. Stavely's poems and short stories reveal themes of lonely isolation, of alienation from the present, and a yearning for days gone by.

THE JEFFERSON·
ISLANDS CLUB, INC.

In the Spring of 1929 a group of prominent Democrats who enjoyed hunting, fishing, and the outdoor life acquired a retreat—two islands in sight of the mainland near Tilghman Island in the Bay Hundred district of Talbot County. Their purpose was to make the islands a "mecca for Democrats" where, in beautiful secluded surroundings, conferences could be held, and communion with the great outdoors in various sporting pursuits.

Originally the Poplar Islands, their name was changed to the Jefferson Islands at the Democrats' request by special Act of the Legislature in Maryland. This was done to conform to the club's stated purpose of "supporting, defending and advancing the fundamental principles of government enunciated by Thomas Jefferson" and "to provide a Club House with

View of Poplar Islands' natural harbor from the clubhouse.

suitable surroundings and comforts where members may assemble, discuss and promote Jeffersonian philosophies . . ."

Franklin D. Roosevelt held court under a mulberry tree, Harry S. Truman hooked rockfish, and senators, congressmen, and industrial tycoons enjoyed this haven for sportsmen. Tallulah Bankhead, daughter of William B. Bankhead, Speaker of the House, is said to have shot two red foxes on the run. Three duck blinds offered fine shooting in the marshes, while facilities for skeet shooting, rifle, and pistol practice were available to members. An endless variety of small game, fish, and shellfish abounded on and around the island.

Specialties of the house offered by proprietors, Varnon and Alice Haddaway, included leg of lamb and a variety of seafood. When their daughter, Mary Jane, spilled peas down Harry Truman's back he graciously responded, "Aw, hell, Honey, don't worry about it; you'll have a story to tell your grandchildren."

At a special "Seafood Outing" on September 22 and 23, 1945, 600 people gathered to honor the late President Roosevelt's assistant, James M. Barnes. Their repast included a side of barbecued beef, home cured hams, and potato salad. Thirty bartenders were hired to serve 500 cases of beer, 300 cases of rye whiskey, 15 cases of bourbon, and 100 cases of scotch donated for the occasion. To cap things off, Truman entertained at the piano while Morton Downey, Sr. sang.

The club lasted on Jefferson Islands for about 15 years. After a fire gutted the clubhouse in 1946, it was closed and the Democrats moved on. They purchased St. Catherine's Island at the confluence of the Potomac and Wicomico Rivers, 59 miles from Washington, D.C., where the club still exists today.

ALICE HADDAWAY'S BAKED ROCKFISH

"Rock" is a native of Chesapeake Bay and the State Fish of Maryland; elsewhere it is called striped bass. Unfavorable environmental habitat, coupled with overharvesting, led to a ban on catching them in 1982. The penalty for rockfish possession is a possible $500 fine and/or or two years in prison. This dish was often served at the Jefferson Islands Club and is recorded here in anticipation of the day when the ban is lifted.

1 tablespoon butter or margarine
1 whole rockfish (approximately 3 pounds), cleaned
1 small onion, sliced
3 slices bacon
Salt and pepper to taste
1 tablespoon minced parsley
1 lemon, sliced

Oven 350°   Serves 6

Place fish in a buttered baking dish. Arrange onion slices down length of fish. Place bacon slices over onion; tuck ends under fish. Season with salt and pepper; sprinkle parsley over all. Bake about 30 minutes or until flesh of the fish parts easily from the bone. Serve with lemon slices.

DODSON FAMILY PICNIC

Turn-of-the-Century

Dodson House, on the grounds of the Chesapeake Bay Maritime Museum, serves today as administrative offices and contains the Howard I. Chapelle Memorial Library. The graceful three-story home was built in the mid-1800s and remained in the Dodson family for several generations. Originally descendants of shipowners and captains, the Dodson family settled in Talbot County about 1700. Richard Slicer Dodson became a well-known Maryland state senator who retired to St. Michaels and lived in Dodson House until 1961.

CINNAMON JUMBLES

A Christmas tradition in the Dodson family since 1894, rose water is the special ingredient in these cinnamony rolled and cut-out cookies. (Rose water may be found in gourmet food shops, bath toiletry shops, and can be made in many pharmacies.)

1/2 pound butter	1/2 teaspoon baking soda
1 tablespoon solid vegetable shortening	1/2 teaspoon cream of tartar
1 pound dark brown sugar	3 eggs
2 ounces cinnamon	2 ounces rose water
1 teaspoon baking powder	5 cups flour
	Granulated sugar

Oven 350°   Yield: About 6 dozen cookies

In a large mixing bowl cream together first seven ingredients. With an electric mixer beat in eggs and rose water; beat in flour until dough is too stiff to use mixer. Blend in remaining flour by hand until dough is no longer sticky. Roll out in white granulated sugar; sprinkle with sugar after rolling; cut in shapes and place on greased baking sheets. Bake 8 to 10 minutes. Store in tins to retain freshness.

THE FISHING PARTY

Fishing Party, Tilghman, MD.
Pub. by R. D. North & Co.
Circa 1909

For more than 100 years, sportfishing has been as much a part of Tilghman Island as the watermen whose boats line the docks there.

In earlier, more leisurely times, log canoes took gentlemen in straw hats and shirtsleeves out to the fishing grounds, while their families enjoyed the day back at their summer hotel. The fishermen took along wicker picnic hampers prepared by the hotel cook, packed with fried chicken, cakes, and seasonal fruits.

Today, sportfishing on the Bay has thousands of devotees, and the excitement and adventure of every trip is as memorable now as ever. We sense this in the postcard, written by a turn-of-the-century angler to his fellow office workers in Baltimore: "Went fishing yesterday and pulled in eight croakers and a trout as long as a twelve-inch rule." Even though there were no records broken, it was more than enough to write home about.

42-pound Rockfish

FISHERMAN'S CHOWDER

For extra zing, add dark rum or sherry to taste. A winter-time chowder is made heartier by the addition of half packages of frozen corn, lima beans, and peas. Served with warm bread and a tossed salad, the meal is complete.

2 to 2-1/2 pounds fresh fish
Pinch of salt
Pinch of thyme
2 bay leaves
10–12 whole cloves
10–12 peppercorns
1/4 pound cubed salt pork
3 onions, chopped
6 celery stalks with leaves, chopped
1 green pepper, chopped
1 28-ounce can stewed tomatoes
1 8-ounce can beef consomme
6 small potatoes, skinned, halved, sliced
1/2 cup catsup
2 tablespoons paprika
6 sprigs parsley, minced
Dash worcestershire sauce
Pinch of curry powder (mild)
Juice and pulp of 1 lemon
Cornstarch
Gravy browning
Rum or sherry (optional)

In a large kettle place fish and fishheads; cover with water. Add salt, thyme, bay leaves, cloves, and peppercorns; simmer for 1-1/2 to 2 hours. Remove bones and skin; flake fish.

In a large frying pan, brown salt pork. Add onions, celery, green pepper, tomatoes, consomme, potatoes, catsup, paprika, parsley, worcestershire sauce, and curry powder. Simmer together until vegetables are soft. Add mixture to fish stock. Add lemon juice and pulp. Thicken mixture with cornstarch; color with gravy browning; simmer 20 to 30 minutes more. Add rum or sherry to taste.

St. Michaels on the Miles— Home of the 3 R's: Races, Regattas, and Rendezvous

With water being the main attraction in Talbot County, its beautiful rivers and innumerable creeks and coves have long been a playground for the "messing-about-in-boats" set. Yachtsmen—and women—from all over the world, skippering every kind of water craft imaginable enjoy the splendid cruising and racing grounds of the Miles River.

In the days when log canoes were work boats, informal races developed when watermen sped to shore in order to get the best price for their seafood. Today, the boats are used strictly for racing and have the potential for more spills and thrills than many amusement park rides. Since there is no weighted keel, crew members on the boards must be nimble in sliding up or down them to counter-balance the sails. Should she go over, the crew has no choice but to wait for a tow back to shore.

HOOPER STRAIT LIGHT

I*n Dorchester County, Hooper Strait is located between Bloodsworth Island on the south, and Hooper's Island and Bishops Head to the north. As the most direct route into Tangier Sound, the lighthouse served admirably as a guide through the narrow, crooked strait and into the Nanticoke and Wicomico Rivers.*

September 14, 1867
Original lighthouse lit and put into operation.

January 11, 1877
Massive ice floes carried the lighthouse away. Structure found several days later five miles downriver in water up to its roofline. The lens, lamp, a bed, and some other furniture items were salvaged.

October 15, 1879
New lighthouse construction completed near the original location, four and one-half miles offshore.

December 2, 1954
Lighthouse converted to a battery-powered, unattended light. Structure boarded up and left to deteriorate.

1958
Lighthouse Board, under U.S. Treasury Department jurisdiction, decided to remove the lighthouse due to expense of

upkeep, and replace it with a skeleton tower.

Early 1966
Coast Guard declared the lighthouse "surplus property" and scheduled it for demolition. The 18-month-old Chesapeake Bay Maritime Museum purchased the lighthouse for $1,000 from the man who was to demolish it. After much red tape, approval was granted to move the lighthouse 60 miles up the Bay to St. Michaels on the Miles River.

November 4, 1966
Lighthouse ceased operations at Hooper Strait location.

November 5, 1966
Originally scheduled moving day. Northwest winds at 30 knots and rough seas caused a delay of one day.

November 6, 1966
Moving Day! Lighthouse, cut in half, is lifted by crane onto

barge and with the tug, *Fisher 11*, started its northward journey.

November 7, 1966
Docking completed at St. Michaels. The trip was termed "smooth and uneventful" by the crew of the tug.

Children were let out of school and townspeople gathered to witness the exciting reassembly of the lighthouse. Lifted by crane, the bottom section was swung from the barge and cheers went up as it was placed on its new steel foundation—complete with the osprey nest on the roof of the attached privy. The moving crew had painstakingly preserved every stick and feather of the mighty fish hawk's nest.

May 20, 1967
RESTORED LIGHTHOUSE OPEN TO THE PUBLIC.

TYPICAL LIGHTHOUSE PROVISIONS FOR ONE YEAR, 1870, *per man:*

One lighthouse keeper claims to have stayed sane by " . . . fishing, tying flies for fishing and perfecting a recipe for bread that requires no yeast."

200 pounds beef	4 bushels potatoes
100 pounds pork	1 bushel onions
1 barrel flour	50 pounds sugar
25 pounds rice	24 pounds coffee
10 gallons beans	4 gallons vinegar

Provisions were provided by the Lighthouse Establishment Board. Supply boat tenders came by three or four times a year with supplies for the keepers. In addition to these rations, keepers often purchased fresh local fruits, vegetables, and dairy products. Their friends, the watermen, stopped by with fresh seafood to share.

With an overflowing seafood market just 20 feet below them, keepers also supplemented their menus with fresh fish caught from the deck of the lighthouse. Bill Greenwood, Assistant Keeper on the Hooper Strait Lighthouse in about 1949 recalled catching a 70-pound drum fish.

THE CHESAPEAKE BAY MARITIME MUSEUM

*Preserving the Heritage of the Bay
through Education and Entertainment*

In the beginning the Indians called it *Chesepiook* . . . "Great Shellfish Bay," and today the Chesapeake remains Maryland's greatest resource. "Dedicated to the collection, preservation, and exhibition of artifacts relating to the Bay and to the history of our ancestors who worked and lived along its 5,000 mile tidewater shoreline," the Museum has been a non-profit, educational institution since 1968. The Museum was first conceived in 1963 as a special project of the Historical Society of Talbot County, which authorized $50,000 to be raised for its establishment in St. Michaels, Maryland. A cadre of enthusiastic volunteers dedicated to preserving the history and traditions of the Bay, raised the money and started restoration of Dodson House, the Museum's first exhibit building. By July, 1965, the Museum's collection had already spilled over into Eagle House, and by October of that year, over 10,000 visitors had come to see the Museum and 540 members were on the books.

By May, 1966, the Museum had purchased the Jewett property (1.3 acres) which

held a large defunct crab house. This was the first of six property acquisitions on Navy Point. The crab house was razed to make way for the abandoned Hooper Strait Lighthouse which the U.S. Government had condemned. The lighthouse was purchased from the demolition contractor for $1,000, moved by barge 60 miles up the Bay, and re-positioned on Navy Point. This cottage-type lighthouse was the inspiration for the Museum's logo, and its light flashes the Morse Code for "CBMM."

Between 1966 and '68 other acquisitions were made by the Museum, including Miss Freedom (on long-term loan from the Naval Academy), the fog bell tower with its original 1,000-lb. bell from Point Lookout, the Webb House (now the Museum Store), the *Barnegat* (*ex-Lightship No. 79*) and the last Chesapeake sloop to retain her original appearance, the *J.T. Leonard*. The Museum's aquarium was also built during this same period of time.

By 1968, it became clear that the Museum's objectives differed from those of the Historical Society, and the Museum was independently incorporated as a private, non-profit educational institution. The board recruited S. Paul Johnston, retired director of the National Air and Space Museum at the Smithsonian Institution, on a part-time basis to supervise the Museum's collections, volunteers, and part-time staff. In 1971, R. J. Holt became the Museum's full-time director and immediately set out to obtain accreditation for the Museum and to acquire, consolidate, and stabilize Museum property. After a lengthy, often tedious process of bringing the Museum up to American Association of Museums' standards, accreditation was granted in March, 1978. By that time the Museum had also acquired the remaining pieces of Navy Point that were owned by others, as well as properties along Museum Road, and a major part of the historical Perry Cabin Farm which had once belonged to purser Samuel Hambleton, who served with Oliver Hazard Perry. This latter property is now the site of the new Propulsion Building and the Fogg's Landing complex of historic houses.

Some buildings on Navy Point were restored; those beyond restoration were demolished. Bulkheading and fill were completed in 1974, as was the Museum's marine railway. Also in 1974, the Museum's first totally new building, the Rouse Memorial Building, which houses the waterfowl collections and the notorious battery and punt guns described in James Michener's novel *Chesapeake* was opened. In 1977 the Amish-built Boat Shop was added, and in 1978

renovations to the Small Boat Shed (originally a steamboat/railroad terminal located in nearby Claiborne) were done, also with the assistance of the Amish. More than 20 of the finest examples of small work and pleasure boats indigenous to the Bay, plus an exhibit on seafood harvesting, are found in the Small Boat Shed. This outstanding collection ranges from an Indian dugout canoe to a five-log oyster tonging canoe and several one-design racing sloops which are archetypes of their respective classes. In the Boat Shop visi-

Navy Point as it appeared before becoming home to the Chesapeake Bay Maritime Museum. The old steamboat wharf is located just behind the tall pilings.

tors can observe the craft of traditional wooden boat building as it is practiced today by the skilled shipwrights who restore and maintain the Museum's historic work boats and other vessels.

The Bay of Chesapeake Building, finished in 1980, was designed to resemble a typical colonial residence from the outside, with its gambrel roof and colonial colors. From the inside, however, 24-foot ceilings allow the display of a crabbing skiff under full sail. Numerous boat models, paintings, and illustrations interpret the geological and cultural past of the Bay from pre-historic times to our own era, with special artifacts highlighting each exhibit area.

In 1979, the five-year task of restoring the bugeye, *Edna E. Lockwood*, was completed, and since then the Museum has continued to restore and maintain other traditional Bay boats like the skipjack *Rosie Parks*, the five-log motor canoe *Alverta*, the oyster dredger *Old Point*, and the Hooper Island Draketail *Martha*.

The Tolchester Beach Bandstand, a delightful structure that recalls the gentility of the Victorian era, was added to the Museum grounds in 1984 and now serves as a focal point for summer concerts. As the Museum has grown in its physical plant, so has its number of exhibits, activities, festivals, and educational programs.

When Jim Holt retired in 1987, the Museum board appointed a new director, John R. Valliant, whose family settled in the St. Michaels District of Talbot County in the late 1600s. The Museum has expanded its special events and educational activities which now include the following annual events: Springfest, Big Band Night, Crab Day, the Kiltie Band Concert, Museum Days, the Mid-Atlantic Small Craft Festival, Oyster Day, and hunting demonstrations during the Waterfowl Festival. The Museum also offers a myriad of environmental and ecological programs, maritime seminars, hands-on nautical skill building classes, and recreational activities such as sailing and fishing in a quasi-classroom environment—all with the overall goal of *Fun That Teaches*!

Current membership is almost 5,000—and growing; visitors to the Museum number over 80,000 annually; and perhaps most unusual, nearly 300 active volunteers assist in virtually every aspect of Museum operations.

NEGUS PUNCH
Mulled Wine

Negus Punch is named for Colonel Francis Negus, d. 1732, the originator. This punch has traditionally been served at the annual Volunteer Association Christmas parties at the Chesapeake Bay Maritime Museum.

The brew is concocted in front of a fireplace. The ingredients which have been previously heated, are poured into a large earthenware bowl and stirred with a red hot poker pulled from the fire. This produces a spectacular burst of steam with an intriguing aroma. It partially caramelizes the sweetened brew, brings the punch up to temperature, and is the signal that the fortified concoction is ready to serve. Those who have imbibed this heady brew attest to its potency.

To 1 quart boiling water in a large ceramic pot add the following ingredients and simmer for 15 minutes:

SYRUP
2 cups sugar
2 dozen whole cloves
12 sticks cinnamon
2 tablespoons grated nutmeg
12 lemons, juice and rinds

Before adding the spirits, strain, reheat and test for flavor/sweetness.

4 quarts madeira or tawny port
1.75 liters vodka
2 seedless oranges, thinly sliced

In a separate pot, combine madeira or tawny port and vodka. Heat well. Combine with the hot syrup solution in the ceramic pot. Float orange slices on top. Stir with a red-hot poker and serve very hot.

MUSEUM SCENES

Clockwise from center: *The tug,* Delaware; *Paul Curtis, Dockmaster; administration buildings, Higgins House and Dodson House; aerial view of Navy Point and St. Michaels Harbor; deadeye and lanyard on* Edna E. Lockwood.

BALTIMORE STEAM PACKET CO.
CELEBRATES CENTENNIAL

This commemorative plate was commissioned for the centennial celebration of the Baltimore Steam Packet Co. The border depicts five representative steamers used between Baltimore and Norfolk from the beginning in 1815 to the present. The first Old Bay Line Steamboat is the Georgia in 1840. During its existence over 100 years the Old Bay Line owned and operated some 48 steamers.

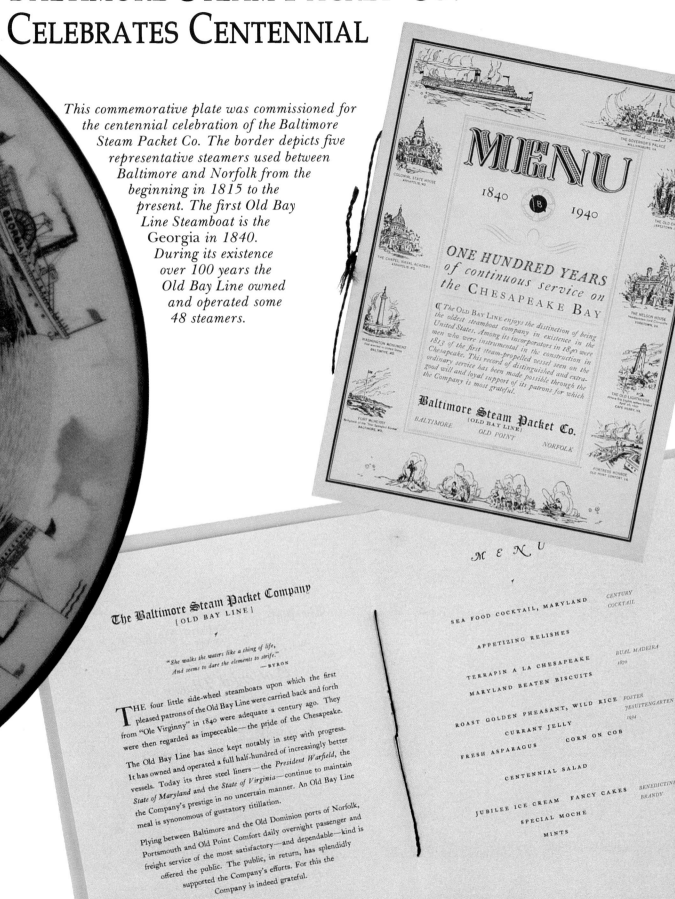

MENU

1840 · B · 1940

ONE HUNDRED YEARS
of continuous service on the CHESAPEAKE BAY

The OLD BAY LINE enjoys the distinction of being the oldest steamboat company in existence in the United States. Among its incorporators in 1840 were men who were instrumental in the construction in 1813 of the first steam-propelled vessel seen on the Chesapeake. This record of distinguished and extra-ordinary service has been made possible through the good will and loyal support of its patrons for which the Company is most grateful.

Baltimore Steam Packet Co.
[OLD BAY LINE]

BALTIMORE — OLD POINT — NORFOLK

The Baltimore Steam Packet Company
[OLD BAY LINE]

*"She walks the waters like a thing of life,
And seems to dare the elements to strife."*
— BYRON

THE four little side-wheel steamboats upon which the first pleased patrons of the Old Bay Line were carried back and forth from "Ole Virginny" in 1840 were adequate a century ago. They were then regarded as impeccable — the pride of the Chesapeake.

The Old Bay Line has since kept notably in step with progress. It has owned and operated a full half-hundred of increasingly better vessels. Today its three steel liners — the *President Warfield*, the *State of Maryland* and the *State of Virginia* — continue to maintain the Company's prestige in no uncertain manner. An Old Bay Line meal is synonomous of gustatory titillation.

Plying between Baltimore and the Old Dominion ports of Norfolk, Portsmouth and Old Point Comfort daily overnight passenger and freight service of the most satisfactory — and dependable — kind is offered the public. The public, in return, has splendidly supported the Company's efforts. For this the Company is indeed grateful.

MENU

SEA FOOD COCKTAIL, MARYLAND	CENTURY COCKTAIL
APPETIZING RELISHES	
TERRAPIN A LA CHESAPEAKE	BUAL MADEIRA 1870
MARYLAND BEATEN BISCUITS	
ROAST GOLDEN PHEASANT, WILD RICE	FOSTER JESUITENGARTEN 1934
CURRANT JELLY	CORN ON COB
FRESH ASPARAGUS	
CENTENNIAL SALAD	
JUBILEE ICE CREAM FANCY CAKES	BENEDICTINE BRANDY
SPECIAL MOCHE	
MINTS	

Trailboards:
From the log canoe, Fly; *the skipjacks* Rosie Parks *and* Robert L. Webster; *and, the oyster sloop,* J. T. Leonard

Navigational Aids for Measuring Latitude:
Backstaff, developed in 1594; Quadrant, circa 1755

Rudder:
From the Robert L. Webster, *the largest skipjack ever built—Length, 60 feet; breadth, 20.3 feet; rudder on exhibit measures 10 feet top to bottom*

Miss Freedom

EDNA E. LOCKWOOD

*Double-ended 9-log Bugeye
ketch with patent stern*
54 feet on deck
55 feet at the waterline
17 feet in beam
*Officially licensed on October
5, 1889*

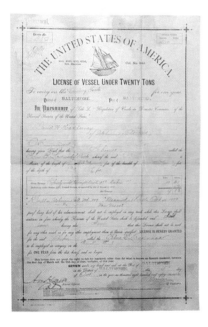

DEMONSTRATIONS, CLASSES, AND EVENTS

Classic Boat Show

Mediterranean Style Mooring

Waterfowl Festival
Bodybooting Method of Hunting, top-center; Punt Gun Demonstration by Ed Lowe and Mark Adams, far right; Decoy Carving by Eric Applegarth

We-Sort Sailing Class

BOAT MAINTENANCE

Brewster Merrill refurbishes
Rosie's *hatches; boatbuilding
class under the tutelage of
Mike Amory; Richard Scofield
retouches the trim on* Martha,
*a Hooper's Island Dovetail, or
Draketail; Richard Scofield
and Lloyd Bayliss maintaining*
Rosie Parks; Rosie Parks
Restored

Kitchen, Hooper Strait Lighthouse

APPETIZERS
AND GROGS

CRAB CAPERS

Deceptively simple—surprisingly unique in flavor.

1 pound backfin crabmeat
1 cup mayonnaise
3/4 cup grated Parmesan cheese
1/2 bottle capers, drained

Combine all ingredients. Place in casserole and bake at 350 degrees for 15 to 20 minutes.

Serve in chafing dish with crackers.

Yield: 6 to 8 appetizer servings

SHRIMP REMOULADE

An elegant appetizer for special occasions.

3 teaspoons dry mustard
4 hard shakes cayenne pepper
Juice of one lemon
2 teaspoons Worcestershire sauce
1 2-inch yellow onion, chopped very fine
2 cloves garlic, chopped very fine
1 cup mayonnaise ♥
2 pounds medium shrimp, cooked and peeled ♥
3 ounces crab seasoning

Combine first seven ingredients in an 8-inch mixing bowl and mix thoroughly.

Place shrimp in large saucepan and cover with cold water. Add 3 ounces of crab seasoning. Heat until water steams (not boils) for 6 minutes. Drain and peel shrimp. Stir into the sauce. Marinate in the refrigerator at least overnight, preferably 24 hours.

Serve on lettuce as an appetizer or in a bowl, to be spooned on stoned wheat crackers, as an hors d'oeuvre.

Prepare in advance.   Yield: 6 to 8 servings

SHRIMP AND CRAB·
COCKTAIL SPREAD

2 8-ounce packages cream cheese
4 tablespoons light cream
1 tablespoon mayonnaise
2 teaspoons lemon juice
1/4 cup onion, finely chopped
1 teaspoon Worcestershire sauce
1/4 teaspoon salt
1/2 cup chili sauce
3 squirts Tabasco sauce
Sprinkle of garlic powder
8 to 10 large shrimp, finely chopped
1 cup crabmeat

Sure to become a neighborhood favorite.

Mix cream cheese, cream and mayonnaise until soft and smooth. Add other ingredients and mix well. Refrigerate.

Serve with potato chips or crackers.

Yield: 8 to 10 appetizer servings

Smoky Bluefish Spread

The author's husband catches bluefish in the Tilghman Island area and smokes them in a covered barbeque over hot coals and a handful of hickory chips.

1/2 pound smoked bluefish, skinned
2 8-ounce packages cream cheese, softened
3 tablespoons minced red or green pepper
3 tablespoons minced onion
2 tablespoons chopped parsley
1 teaspoon Dijon mustard
1/2 teaspoon horseradish
3 drops Tabasco sauce
2 tablespoons sour cream
Salt and pepper to taste

Mix all ingredients and refrigerate. Soften before serving.

Spread on crackers to serve.

Freezes well.   Yield: 1-1/2 pints

Hot Clam Cracker Spread

Quick, easy and delicious any time family and friends gather.

1/4 pound butter (not margarine)
2 6-1/2-ounce cans minced clams with juice
1 cup fine bread crumbs (Italian style preferred)
1 tablespoon dried oregano
1 tablespoon dried parsley flakes
Garlic salt to taste
Pepper to taste
1/4 cup grated Parmesan cheese

Melt butter in oven-proof one-quart dish. Add all ingredients except Parmesan cheese and mix thoroughly. Sprinkle with Parmesan cheese.

Bake at 350 degrees for 15 minutes. Serve with crackers.

Can be prepared ahead   Yield: 6 to 8 appetizer servings
and reheated before serving.

JAMAICAN CRAB DIP

1/4 cup minced onion
1/4 cup sweet pickle relish
1/2 cup mayonnaise
1 cup thick dairy sour cream
2 tablespoons dark Jamaican rum
1 pound lump crabmeat

Dark rum is the secret ingredient in this unique recipe.

Mix first five ingredients together. Gently fold in crabmeat to keep lumps in large pieces. Refrigerate.

Serve on melba toast or crackers.

Can be prepared a day ahead.   Yield: 4 cups

CRUNCHY ORANGE SPREAD

1 medium orange, unpeeled
1 cup broken walnuts *or* pecans
2-1/2 cups light raisins
1/4 teaspoon cinnamon
1/2 to 3/4 cup mayonnaise or salad dressing

Easy—healthy—delicious—different.

Quarter and seed unpeeled orange. In food processor bowl, process orange and nuts until finely chopped. Add half the raisins, the cinnamon and mayonnaise or salad dressing. Process until finely chopped. Add remaining raisins and process again until finely chopped.

Serve on crackers, orange slices, or celery sticks. Store chilled in a covered container or freeze up to 3 months.

Yield: 4 cups

ARTICHOKE FONDUE

A versatile dish, excellent heated and served over pasta, sprinkled with Parmesan cheese and crumbled bacon, if desired. Also, a surprise topping for baked potatoes.

1 3-ounce package cream cheese, softened
1/2 cup mayonnaise
3/4 cup dairy sour cream
1 tablespoon Worcestershire sauce
1 cup grated sharp Cheddar cheese
1 14-ounce can artichoke hearts, drained and chopped
3 scallions, including some of the tops, finely chopped
1 4-ounce can chopped green chilies (optional)

Combine all ingredients in a medium-size mixing bowl. Place mixture in a casserole; cover and bake 30 minutes at 350 degrees.

Serve with crackers, chips or fresh vegetable crudites.

Yield: 2-1/2 cups

GOLDEN CHEESE PUFF

Fancy as a souffle, but without the fuss.

6 slices firm white bread, crusts removed
1 pound Havarti cheese, coarsley grated
1-1/2 cups milk
2 dashes Tabasco
3 eggs
1 loaf French bread

Cut bread slices into thirds. In a buttered 1-1/2-quart-baking dish, arrange half the bread slices, then half the grated cheese. Repeat, using remaining bread slices and cheese.

Whisk together milk, Tabasco and eggs. Pour over bread-cheese layers and allow to stand at room temperature for 30 minutes. Bake in preheated 350-degree oven for 25 to 30 minutes, until golden and puffy.

Serve hot, spread on thin slices of fresh French bread.

Yield: 8 appetizer servings

CRAB IN A CAP

1 pound crabmeat (or combination of chopped shrimp, scallops, lobster and/or clams)

1/2 cup thick white sauce seasoned with 1/2 garlic clove, 1/4 teaspoon thyme, salt and cracked pepper

1/2 cup mayonnaise

1/4 cup butter

1 cup fresh mushroom stems, sliced

1/2 cup celery, diced

Dash Tabasco sauce

1/2 tablespoon Worcestershire sauce

1 tablespoon lemon juice

1/2 cup dried bread crumbs

3 to 4 dozen bite-size mushroom caps

1/2 cup white wine

Slices of provolone cheese, cut into bite-size pieces

Mix seafood, seasoned white sauce and mayonnaise.

Sauté mushroom stem slices and celery in butter until tender. Add to seafood mixture. Add Tabasco sauce, Worcestershire sauce, lemon juice and bread crumbs. Mix thoroughly.

Stuff mushroom caps with mixture and arrange in a large baking dish. Pour wine around mushroom caps and bake at 350 degrees until hot, about 25 minutes, basting with wine several times.

When caps are tender and seafood is hot, top with cheese and broil until cheese bubbles. Serve at once.

Yield: 10 to 12 appetizer servings

Quite possibly the world's best stuffed mushrooms.

Oysters à la Henny

The author adapted this recipe from one prepared by close family friends, who cooked it in their woodstove. His version—broiling the oysters in their shells—combines easy preparation and attractive presentation.

12 Chesapeake Bay oysters in shell
1-1/2 teaspoons horseradish
Tabasco sauce
Worcestershire sauce
3 slices sharp Cheddar cheese
3 slices bacon

Shuck oysters, letting oyster remain in deep half of shell. Arrange oysters in a single layer in a foil-lined shallow baking pan.

Top each oyster with 1/8 teaspoon horseradish, a drop of hot pepper sauce, 2 drops of Worcestershire sauce, one-quarter slice of cheese. Top with one-quarter slice of bacon.

Place pan about 6 inches from heat and broil 5 minutes or until bacon is crisp.

Yield: 4 appetizer servings

Italian Sausage Balls

This "old family favorite" is quite up-to-date in its zesty use of red pepper. Adjust the amount for tamer tastes.

5 pounds lean pork butt, ground
1 teaspoon salt per pound
3/4 teaspoon fennel seed per pound
1/2 teaspoon crushed ground red pepper per pound
3/4 teaspoon black pepper per 5 pounds (1 teaspoon per 10 pounds)
Paprika for color
Water
4 quarts spaghetti sauce

Have your butcher grind the pork butt.

Mix together seasonings and sprinkle this mixture over ground pork. Mix well. While mixing, add approximately half a glass of water per 5 pounds.

When ingredients are well mixed, cover bowl and refrigerate for 2 to 3 hours. This will make the meat easier to form into balls.

Form chilled sausage mixture into bite-size balls. Drop into simmering spaghetti sauce and cook until sausage balls are cooked through, 2 hours or longer. (Further cooking improves flavor.)

Serve sausage balls in spaghetti sauce in a chafing dish.

Can be frozen in small batches

Yield: 250 to 300 appetizer-size balls

GOOM BAY SMASH

16 ounces pineapple juice

8 ounces orange juice

7 ounces coconut rum or liqueur

7 ounces banana rum or liqueur

7 ounces gold rum

3 ounces apricot brandy

A favorite raft-up drink of the Sailing Club of Washington (SCOW). They suggest that it be enjoyed with caution—it is lethal!

Mix all ingredients in a large pitcher. Serve over ice.

Yield: Six 8-ounce servings

AMARETTO SUNSHINE

1/3 cup orange juice concentrate

1/3 cup water

1/4 cup sugar

1/4 teaspoon vanilla

1/2 cup milk

5 ounces Amaretto

Enjoy this "sunshine" day or night.

Fill blender with ice; add all ingredients and liquefy.

Yield: 4 servings

RUM ROSIE

In honor of the Museum's skipjack, Rosie Parks, *this original grog recipe was created for the collection. In the best of maritime tradition, dark rum is combined with scurvy-preventing lime juice. The addition of pink lemonade and peach schnapps produces a thirst-quenching elixir to lift your spirits.*

1 ounce dark rum
1 ounce peach schnapps
1 wedge of lime
8 ounces pink lemonade

Combine rum and peach schnapps in a 12-ounce glass. Squeeze juice from lime wedge into glass and add lime wedge. Fill glass with ice and pink lemonade.

Yield: One 12-ounce glass

1 pint dark rum
1 pint peach schnapps
Juice of two limes
4 quarts pink lemonade
Lime slices for garnish

Combine all ingredients in a large punch bowl. Serve over ice.

Yield: 5 quarts

DINING ASHORE AND AFLOAT

MaryAnn McNamara-Ringwald

GRILLED PORK ROAST

Vacuum-packed pork tenderloins stay fresh throughout a week's cruise. They make an excellent last-night-out barbeque dinner.

2-pound boneless pork roast ♥
3 tablespoons brown mustard
1/4 cup Tamari or soy sauce

Slather mustard on both sides of pork and marinate in Tamari for at least 1 hour. Turn once or twice.

Grill on hot closed grill or boat barbeque for 20 minutes on each side, or until done to your taste. Adjust time to larger or smaller piece of meat. Best if not over-cooked and still juicy.

Yield: 4 servings

Low-Cholesterol Conversion:
Substitute a 2-pound whole turkey breast, skinned and de-boned, for pork. Prepare as above.

PIQUANT CHICKEN MEDALLIONS

Easy enough for shipboard preparation and fancy enough for special guests.

2 8-ounce chicken breasts, skin removed
Flour
3 tablespoons butter ♥
1/4 cup thinly sliced mushrooms
25-30 large capers
1 cup dry white wine
Bay leaf
Salt and pepper to taste
1/4 cup chicken stock ♥
Chopped parsley

Bone each chicken breast, separating tenderloin, and cut each breast into six medallions. Dust lightly with flour. Melt butter and sauté mushrooms with half the capers. In the same mixture, sauté chicken breast pieces until golden brown. Remove and set aside.

Deglaze pan by adding white wine, additional capers and bay leaf, bringing to rapid boil and scraping the pan. Season to taste. Allow to bubble until reduced by half.

Pour a light layer of sauce over breasts. Stir chicken stock into remaining sauce mixture. Heat and pour additional sauce over chicken. Sprinkle with parsley.

Yield: 3 servings

Low-Cholesterol Conversion:
Substitute 2 tablespoons margarine for 3 tablespoons butter; use vegetable oil cooking spray along with margarine to brown chicken breasts and sauté mushrooms. Add 1 tablespoon fresh lemon juice along with white wine and degreased chicken stock.

MOLLY'S CHICKEN CANTON

3-1/2 pounds frying chicken, cut into pieces

4 tablespoons butter or margarine

1 large onion, quartered and separated into layers

1 green pepper, cut into strips

1 16-ounce can sliced peaches, undrained

2 tablespoons cornstarch

2 tablespoons soy sauce

6 tablespoons vinegar

2 medium tomatoes, cut in sixths

This recipe honors the cook, Molly, and the seafaring pup, Canton, who became the original ancestor of today's Chesapeake Bay retrievers.

Brown chicken in butter. Cover and cook just until tender. Remove from skillet and keep warm. Add onion and pepper to skillet and cook until onion is transparent. Remove and keep warm.

Drain syrup from peaches into skillet. Stir in cornstarch, soy sauce, and vinegar and cook until clear and slightly thickened. Return chicken, onion and pepper to skillet.

Add peaches and tomatoes to skillet and cook 5 minutes more. Serve hot over rice.

Yield: 6 servings

•Boat Chicken

So named because vegetable ingredients are likely to be carried aboard.

1 chicken, skinned and cut into pieces
1 bunch fresh basil *or* 1 tablespoon dried basil
2 10-ounce cans chicken broth
4 carrots, cut in slices
4 new potatoes
3/4 pound fresh green beans (optional)
2 small onions, quartered
3 tablespoons butter
3 tablespoons flour
1/4 cup Dijon mustard
1/3 cup cream, sour cream, yogurt, or milk
Salt and pepper to taste

Bring chicken pieces to a boil in chicken broth seasoned with basil. Simmer 15 minutes. Add potatoes and carrots and simmer for 20 minutes. Add onions and beans and simmer for 10 to 15 minutes or until all ingredients are tender.

Melt butter, add flour and whisk without browning for 2 or 3 minutes. Add chicken broth from main dish and whisk until smooth. Whisk in mustard and cream.

Spoon sauce over the chicken and vegetables and serve with rice.

Yield: 4 servings

•Lori Cacciatore

Delicious and very versatile— vegetables can be changed according to what you have on hand. Par-boiled potatoes with fresh parsley may be added to the dish before baking, and you have a complete meal in one dish.

4 chicken breast halves
1/2 cup white wine Worcestershire sauce
1 large green pepper
1 medium apple
1 cup pearl onions (*or* one large onion, sliced)
8 to 10 mushrooms, cut in half
Fresh ground pepper to taste
1/4 cup raisins (optional)

Marinate chicken breasts in Worcestershire sauce 4 hours or overnight.

Place chicken in baking dish, reserving Worcestershire sauce. Slice pepper; cut each slice into fourths and place in dish. Core and cut apple in quarters and add along with onions and mushrooms.

Pour Worcestershire sauce over all ingredients. Add pepper and raisins and cover. Bake at 350 degrees for approximately 45 minutes.

Yield: 4 servings

GLAZED LONDON BROIL

1 flank steak (2 to 2-1/2 pounds)
2 teaspoons unseasoned meat tenderizer
1 tablespoon sugar
2 tablespoons dry sherry
2 tablespoons soy sauce
1 tablespoon honey
1 teaspoon salt

Equally tasty grilled over the transom or in the backyard.

Pierce surfaces of flank steak at 1-inch intervals with a sharp fork. Combine remaining ingredients and pour over steak. Let stand at room temperature 1 hour, turning occasionally.

Broil with surface of meat about 3 inches from source of heat, allowing about 3 minutes for each side. This will be rare, so allow longer if you want it well done. (Watch while cooking, as flank steak curls and may burn at curled edges. Make slits with knife to flatten.)

To serve, slice with sharp knife into thin slices, carving at an angle against the grain.

Yield: 8 servings

VEAL SCALLOPS IN BRANDY SAUCE

Any occasion becomes special when you serve this delectable entree.

1 leek, white and yellow part only

1 medium carrot

4 tablespoons butter

3/4 pound veal scallops, pounded lightly

1/3 cup flour seasoned with 1/2 teaspoon salt and 1/8 teaspoon pepper

1/4 cup chicken broth

1/4 cup dry white wine

1/2 cup heavy cream

1-1/2 tablespoons brandy

1/4 cup diced fresh tomato

1/4 teaspoon salt

Wash leek and cut into 2-1/2-inch long julienne. Peel carrot and cut into 2-1/2-inch long julienne. Melt butter in a large skillet. Sauté the carrot and leek in the butter until they are just tender. Remove vegetables from butter and keep warm.

Cut veal into pieces approximately 2 × 3 inches. Dredge in seasoned flour and shake off excess. Increase heat under skillet to medium-high. Sauté veal in butter until just tender, turning once—about 3 to 4 minutes. Remove from skillet and keep warm in a 200-degree oven.

Deglaze skillet with broth and wine, scraping up brown bits. Bring to a boil and reduce to 1/4 cup. Add cream and brandy. Reduce over medium-high heat about 4 minutes, until the sauce just coats a spoon. Add tomato and salt. Simmer 1 minute.

To serve, top scallops with sauce. Strew julienne vegetables over top. Serve hot.

Yield: 4 servings

After-The-Wedding-Stew

2 tablespoons oil
2 teaspoons margarine
6- to 8-pound leg of lamb, cut into cubes
2 cups chopped onion
2 cloves garlic, minced
1/4 cup flour
1 teaspoon salt
1/4 teaspoon pepper
2 cups white wine
2 8-ounce cans tomato sauce
2 13-3/4 ounce cans chicken broth
1/4 cup fresh parsley, chopped
1 bay leaf
1/2 teaspoon thyme
2 cups bite-size pieces of fresh carrots
1 10-ounce package frozen tiny onions
2 cups frozen peas, cooked and drained

This stew has been traditionally served to family and close friends after the reception is over and the last guest has left.

Heat oil and margarine in a large skillet. Brown meat in small batches and transfer to large Dutch oven.

Add chopped onion and garlic to skillet, and sprinkle with flour, salt and pepper. Mix well. Add wine and bring to a boil. Stir until sauce starts to thicken, scraping up brown bits from bottom of skillet. Stir in tomato sauce, broth, parsley, bay leaf and thyme. Bring to a boil.

Pour onion mixture over browned meat in Dutch oven. Bake at 350 degrees for 1-1/2 hours, until meat is tender. Add onions and carrots, and discard bay leaf. Bake for 15 minutes, until vegetables are done. Warm pre-cooked peas.

Transfer stew to serving dish, sprinkle with peas, and serve with rice or noodles.

Can be prepared in advance.   Yield: 8 to 10 servings

WINDRUSH LEG OF LAMB

A feast for the eye as well as the palate.

1 butterflied leg of lamb, fell left on
1 teaspoon dried rosemary
2 teaspoons minced garlic
1/2 teaspoon dried thyme
Salt and pepper
Vegetable oil
1/4 pound fresh spinach
4 medium carrots, peeled and cooked whole
1/2 medium onion, sliced thin
1/4 cup minced parsley

Pat meat dry and sprinkle with seasonings and a few drops of vegetable oil. Cover meat with a layer of spinach. Arrange carrots in two rows and put onions and parsley on top. Roll up and tie very securely.

Roast at 325 degrees for 1-1/2 hours. Allow to stand 15 minutes before slicing.

Yield: 6 to 8 servings, according to size of leg of lamb

SEAGOING SCAMPI

A great galley dish—simple and fast.

1 pound shrimp, shelled and deveined
1 pound scallops
5 tablespoons olive oil
Dash Worcestershire sauce
3 garlic cloves, minced
3 scallions, minced
1/2 cup fresh parsley, minced
1/4 cup white wine or sherry
2 teaspoons lemon juice

Sauté shrimp and scallops in 3 tablespoons olive oil until shrimp turn pink. Remove and keep warm.

Add to pan 2 tablespoons oil, Worcestershire sauce, minced garlic, scallions, and parsley. Sauté about 3 minutes; add wine or sherry, seafood and lemon juice. Sauté briefly to heat, about 2 minutes. Serve with rice.

Note: Small lobster pieces may be substituted for shrimp and scallops.

Yield: 4 servings

BARBEQUED SHRIMP AU JUS

2 pounds raw shrimp, shelled and deveined ♥

Succulent grilled shrimp are lavished with two sauces.

BASTING SAUCE:
1/4 pound butter ♥
Juice of one lemon
1 teaspoon Worcestershire sauce

AU JUS SAUCE:
1 10-ounce can beef bouillon
1/4 teaspoon garlic powder
1/2 teaspoon onion powder
1/4 teaspoon celery salt
Pinch of thyme

Thread shrimp equally on 6 skewers so that the back of one shrimp lies into the belly of the preceding shrimp.

Basting sauce: Melt butter and combine with lemon juice and Worcestershire sauce.

Au jus sauce: In a small skillet, combine beef bouillon and spices. Boil down to 2/3 of the original volume.

Barbeque the skewers of shrimp over a fairly hot charcoal fire, turning and basting frequently for about 5 minutes. The shrimp should be lightly browned and a little charred on the outside. Use all the basting sauce, but DO NOT overcook.

Place skewers on serving plates. Spoon a couple of ounces of the beef sauce over each skewer and serve hot.

Yield: 6 servings

ISLAND SUPPER SALAD

This unusual do-ahead dish makes a cool supper for a summer night on the Bay.

1-1/2 cups mayonnaise ♥
1/4 to 1/2 cup horseradish, well drained
1 teaspoon garlic powder
2 teaspoons dry mustard
2 teaspoons lemon juice
1/2 teaspoon salt
Beau Monde seasoning
10 ounces cooked bay scallops (*or* quartered large
   scallops)
1 head raw cauliflower, broken into bite-size buds
1 pound small mushrooms, whole
1-1/2 to 2 pounds cooked shrimp, peeled ♥
1 box small cherry tomatoes
1 can water chestnuts, cut into thick slices
1 can pitted ripe olives, sliced (optional)
Chopped parsley

Combine first six ingredients, sprinkle with Beau Monde seasoning and mix well. Add remaining ingredients except parsley. Toss gently. Marinate 5 to 6 hours.

Sprinkle with chopped parsley and serve.

Prepare in advance.   Yield: 8 to 10 servings

Low-Cholesterol Conversion:
Substitute 1-1/2 to 2 pounds cooked Sea Legs for shrimp and 1-1/2 cups cholesterol-free mayonnaise. For mushrooms, use 1/2-ounce dried Shitake mushrooms which have been soaked in warm chicken bouillon for 10 minutes and drained. Omit olives. Combine and marinate as above.

Bountiful Bay

THE CLASSIC CRAB CAKE

Every Bay cook has a "best" crab cake recipe. They don't come any better than this.

1 egg
2 heaping tablespoons mayonnaise
1 heaping teaspoon prepared yellow mustard
1 tablespoon cream
Salt and pepper to taste
1 slice bread, toasted and crumbled
1 teaspoon fresh parsley, chopped
1/2 teaspoon Worcestershire sauce
1 pound fresh crabmeat

Mix together all ingredients except crab. Stir in crab and form into 4 patties.

Fry in cooking oil until golden, about 5 minutes on each side.

Yield: 4 servings

THE ULTIMATE CRAB CAKE

A purist's delight, with no "sawdust" to diminish the splendor of pure crabmeat.

1 pound lump crabmeat
1 egg, beaten
Crab seasoning to taste

Mix the ingredients together, seasoning to taste. Form mixture into 2 8-ounce crab cakes.

Place crab cakes on a preheated, oiled frying pan. Cook over medium heat on both sides until browned, approximately 5 to 10 minutes. Serve hot.

Yield: 2 enormous servings

QUICK CRAB IMPERIAL

1/2 cup light cream *or* evaporated milk ♥
3 tablespoons mayonnaise ♥
6 tablespoons butter ♥
1 small onion, minced fine
1/4 green pepper, minced fine
1 tablespoon parsley, chopped
1/2 teaspoon dry mustard
Dash Tabasco
1 pound lump crabmeat
1/2 cup corn flake crumbs
2 tablespoons melted butter ♥

Add a chopped hard-boiled egg and half a cup sliced mushrooms for extra-hearty appetites.

Add cream to mayonnaise in small bowl. Stir well and set aside. Melt butter in pan. Add onion and pepper and simmer 5 minutes. Stir well, then add cream mixture. Add parsley, mustard and Tabasco. Let come to a boil and cook slowly until mixture is smooth and well blended. Cool. Stir in crabmeat.

Place in casserole (or 4 individual baking dishes). Top with corn flake crumbs mixed with melted butter. Bake at 400 degrees for 20 minutes.

Yield: 4 servings

Low-Cholesterol Conversion:
Substitute 1/2 cup evaporated non-fat skim milk, 3 tablespoons no-cholesterol mayonnaise, and 3/4 stick of margarine for first three ingredients. Omit butter from corn flake crumbs; spray with vegetable oil spray instead. Eliminate hard-boiled egg.

CRABS ITALIAN

For a hot summer day, try a hot new way to enjoy Cheasapeake crabs. Just how hot is up to the hand that shakes on the spices.

Extra virgin olive oil

Fresh garlic

One dozen fresh Chesapeake crabs, spray-rinsed and waste discarded

Parsley

Paprika

Salt

Pepper, cayenne, or crushed red pepper to taste

Pepper seeds

Dry white wine

In a large frying pan, pour olive oil to cover bottom. Turn on heat to medium-high. Press 2 or 3 cloves of garlic through a press and add to oil.

When oil is medium hot, place crabs bottom-side up in pan. Sprinkle on healthy doses of parsley and paprika, enough to completely cover bottom side of crabs. Sprinkle on salt, pepper and pepper seeds to taste. Let crabs simmer, turning periodically, until crabs are red-orange and seasoning is brown.

Pour white wine over crabs approximately 1/2 inch deep. Let simmer 5 to 10 minutes. Pour crabs and wine sauce into a serving tray, so crabmeat can be dipped into sauce. For extra heat, add a dash of Tabasco to the sauce.

Crabs can be served directly or chilled in the refrigerator. To reheat, warm crabs gently in oven, being sure meat does not dry out.

Yield: 3 to 4 servings

A MOVABLE CRAB FEAST

Crab seasoning *or* **1 box salt mixed with 4-ounce bottle
red pepper sauce**

1/2 cup vinegar

4 dozen live hard-shell crabs

**1 ice chest big enough to hold 4 dozen crabs
(Styrofoam will not warp)**

Plunge crabs in boiling water with vinegar and very little seasoning. Boil for 11 minutes.

Remove and immediately place (while hot) one layer crabs in bottom of ice chest. Sprinkle generously with crab seasoning. Then place another layer of crabs and seasoning and repeat process of layering until all crabs are placed and covered with seasoning.

Cover with newspaper and close top securely. Heat will steam crabs and melt scasoning for flavor. After 1 hour take out and eat. Crabs will stay hot for 5 or 6 hours.

Note: You can prepare shrimp this same way.

Yield: 48 steamed crabs

This is an excellent way to prepare crabs before your guests arrive, or to make a portable crab feast to take on the boat or to the park.

CREAM OF CRAB SOUP

4 tablespoons butter or margarine

2 tablespoons flour

2 cups milk

1/4 teaspoon salt

1 cup half-and-half

1/4 teaspoon lemon celery seasoning

1 tablespoon chopped parsley

4 tablespoons sherry

1 pound backfin crabmeat

Melt butter and stir in flour. Add milk and salt and bring to a boil.

Add half-and-half, seasonings, sherry, and crabmeat. Heat thoroughly, but do not boil.

Yield: 4 servings

Offer a small cruet of sherry for those who would like an extra splash.

137

MILES RIVER STUFFED SHELLS

Everyone raves about this innovative crab dish, created on the shores of the Miles River.

STUFFING:
1 8-ounce package cream cheese
1/3 cup sour cream
2 tablespoons chopped green pepper
1 teaspoon Worcestershire sauce
3 tablespoons margarine or butter
1/3 cup grated sharp cheese
2 tablespoons chopped onion
1/2 pound crabmeat
1 box jumbo pasta shells, cooked, rinsed, and drained

SAUCE:
4 tablespoons butter or margarine
1/3 cup flour
1 cup clear chicken broth
2 cups milk
1/2 pound crabmeat
Salt and pepper to taste
Crab seasoning to taste (1/4 to 1/2 teaspoon)

TOPPING:
1/2 to 3/4 cup grated sharp cheese
Paprika
Fresh parsley, chopped

Mix first 8 ingredients together and stuff approximately 15 to 20 pasta shells. Place shells in buttered baking pan or casserole dish.

Melt 4 tablespoons butter or margarine in saucepan. Blend in flour and slowly stir in chicken broth. Add 1 cup milk and cook on medium heat, stirring until thick. Slowly add remaining cup of milk, remaining crabmeat and seasonings. Simmer gently for a few minutes. Pour over pasta shells.

Top shells with 1/2 to 3/4 cup grated cheese. Sprinkle with paprika. Bake at 325 degrees approximately 25 minutes until cheese melts and sauce is thick and bubbly. Garnish with parsley before serving.

Yield: 4 to 6 servings

SEAFOOD IMPERIAL

3/4 cup chopped green pepper

3/4 cup chopped onion

1 cup diced celery

1 cup cooked crabmeat

1 cup cooked shrimp

1 cup cooked lobster

2 hard-boiled eggs, chopped

1 teaspoon salt

Cracked pepper to taste

1 tablespoon Worcestershire sauce

1 cup mayonnaise

1/2 cup dairy sour cream

2 tablespoons melted butter

1 cup soft bread crumbs

Chopped parsley

This classic "royal" recipe need not be limited to crabmeat alone.

Mix together all ingredients except crumbs and butter. Place in a 2-quart buttered casserole. Top with buttered crumbs.

Bake at 350 degrees for 30 minutes. Sprinkle with parsley and serve.

Yield: 6 to 8 servings

OXFORD SEAFOOD GUMBO

The authors often enjoy preparing this aboard their sloop as they sail the Chesapeake Bay. The seafood ingredients may be varied depending upon availability and personal preference.

8 tablespoons flour

7 tablespoons oil

2 large onions, chopped

5 stalks celery, chopped

1 large green pepper, chopped

1 medium bunch fresh parsley, chopped

2 cloves garlic, chopped

2 14-1/2-ounce cans whole tomatoes

1 15-ounce can tomato sauce

1 6-ounce can tomato paste

2 quarts water

1 cup hearty red wine

2 teaspooons lemon juice

6 seasoned, steamed crabs, cleaned and broken in half

1-1/2 tablespoons salt

Crushed red pepper to taste

1 tablespoon sugar

2 large bay leaves

2 teaspoons Tabasco sauce

1 10-ounce package frozen sliced okra

1 pound backfin crabmeat (picked)

3 pounds medium raw shrimp, peeled and deveined

1 pint select oysters

1 pint Bay scallops

1 teaspoon filé powder

Hot steamed rice

Using a heavy 6-quart pot with a non-stick lining, make a dark roux of flour and oil. Stir with a wooden spoon, watching carefully that roux does not burn.

When roux is dark brown, add onions, celery, green pepper, parsley, and garlic. Stir until vegetables mix with roux and brown slightly. Add juice from tomatoes, tomato sauce, and tomato paste. Crush tomatoes and add slowly with water, wine, and lemon juice.

Bring mixture to a gentle boil, stirring frequently. Add broken crab halves and the seasonings, except filé powder. Continue cooking for 1 hour. Taste and adjust seasonings.

Add sliced okra and cook for another hour. Remove and discard crab halves.

Add shrimp and crabmeat and simmer 15 minutes. Add oysters and scallops and cook an additional 15 minutes. Taste and adjust seasonings.

Add filé powder 15 minutes before serving. If gumbo becomes too thick, thin with wine and water, as necessary.

Serve over hot rice in bowls.

Yield: 15 servings

BUGEYE CHOWDER

1 large red bell pepper, chopped
2-1/2 tablespoons unsalted butter
2 medium onions, chopped
3 small potatoes, peeled and diced
Ground white pepper to taste
1/4 teaspoon dried thyme
1/4 teaspoon dried basil
1 pint oysters, juice drained and reserved
3 8-ounce bottles clam juice
2 cups light cream
1/8 pound shredded, dried, smoked beef
1 12-ounce package frozen shoepeg corn
1-1/2 cups fresh broccoli florets, blanched
Salt to taste

Chipped beef and oysters make unexpected fine mates in this hearty soup.

Sauté red pepper in 1 tablespoon butter until soft. Remove to a dish and reserve.

Add 1-1/2 tablespoons butter to pan and sauté onions over low heat until soft. Add potatoes, stirring gently. Add white pepper, thyme and basil. Stir. Add reserved oyster liquor, clam juice, and cream. Simmer 5 minutes.

Add chipped beef to chowder and simmer 10 minutes more. Add corn, broccoli, and red pepper. Season to taste with salt. Add oysters and cook only until their edges begin to curl. Serve immediately in warm bowls.

Chowder may be made in advance without oysters. Reheat chowder and add oysters just before serving.

Yield: 8 to 10 servings

WILD RICE AND OYSTER CASSEROLE

Colorful and flavorful.

1 5-ounce package wild rice, cooked according to package directions
1 10-ounce package frozen chopped spinach, cooked and drained
1/4 cup butter or margarine, melted
1 quart oysters, drained
Salt and pepper to taste
1 can cream of mushroom soup
8 ounces dairy sour cream
1 small onion, finely chopped
1/2 cup sherry
2 tablespoons curry powder (optional)

Combine cooked wild rice, cooked spinach, and butter. Place half of mixture in a 2-quart casserole.

Cover with oysters and season with salt and pepper. Top with remaining rice and spinach mixture.

Heat soup, undiluted. Add remaining ingredients to soup and pour over rice and oysters. Bake at 325 degrees for 1 hour.

Yield: 6 to 8 servings

COCKADOODLE OYSTERS

Plump oysters and tender chicken share a rich cream sauce.

1/4 cup butter or margarine
1/4 cup minced celery
3 tablespoons flour
1/2 teaspoon salt
2 cups rich milk or half-and-half
1 pint oysters
2 cups cooked chicken breast, cut into walnut-size pieces
2 tablespoons chopped pimento
1 tablespoon chopped parsley

Melt butter and sauté celery in it. Add flour and salt and mix. Add milk and liquor from the oysters. Cook until thick.

Add chicken and heat. At the last minute, add oysters and heat until edges curl. Stir in pimento and parsley, and serve on toast points.

To make toast points, trim crusts from very thin bread. Butter and cut into triangles. Place on a tray in a 200-degree oven for 1/2 hour until light brown.

Yield: 6 servings

OYSTER BISQUE FLORENTINE

1 10-ounce package frozen spinach *or* 12 ounces fresh spinach, stems removed

4 cups chicken stock

1 tablespoon lemon juice

1 teaspoon coarse salt

1/4 teaspoon fresh ground pepper

1/8 teaspoon thyme

1/2 cup chopped onion

1/2 cup chopped celery

1 small clove garlic, minced

3 tablespoons butter or margarine

3 tablespoons flour

1 tablespoon Pernod *or* Ricard liqueur (optional)

1 pint oysters with liquor, cut in half

1 cup heavy cream (heavy is best, light will do)

Lemon slices for garnish

Traditional oyster bisque dresses up with spinach and seasonings for extra color and flavor.

Cook spinach in chicken stock seasoned with lemon juice, salt, pepper, and thyme. Blend or process until pureed. Return to pot.

In a medium skillet, sauté onion, celery and garlic in butter until soft. Sprinkle on flour. Stir over low heat for 3 minutes. Add to spinach pot and simmer about 10 minutes. Add liqueur, if using it.

Add oysters and their liquor to pot. Simmer for 3 minutes. Add cream and simmer for 4 more minutes, until heated well (don't boil after the cream is added). Garnish each bowl with a lemon slice.

Yield: 6 to 8 servings

OYSTER-ARTICHOKE PAN ROAST

Take the chill off a blustery winter evening with this satisfying combination.

1 14-ounce can artichoke hearts, drained and quartered
4 tablespoons butter or margarine ♥
1 cup chopped scallions
1/2 cup chopped onion
1 clove garlic, minced
3 tablespoons flour
1 quart oysters with their liquor
1/2 cup chopped fresh parsley
1 teaspoon Worcestershire sauce
1 tablespoon lemon juice
1/4 teaspoon Tabasco sauce
1/2 teaspoon salt
2 tablespoons butter or margarine
1 cup fresh bread crumbs

Cover artichoke hearts with water and bring to a simmer. Keep warm.

Heat 4 tablespoons butter or margarine in a medium skillet and sauté scallions, onion and garlic until tender. Sprinkle on flour and sauté another 3 minutes to cook flour.

While vegetables are cooking, poach oysters in their liquor (add a little water, if necessary) until edges curl and they plump up. Drain oysters, reserving liquid.

Add 1 to 1-1/2 cups of oyster liquid to vegetables. Add parsley, Worcestershire sauce, lemon juice, Tabasco sauce, and salt. Simmer until thickened. Place oysters and artichokes in shallow casserole and cover with sauce. (Can be prepared ahead of time up to this point.)

Melt 2 tablespoons butter or margarine in skillet and toss with bread crumbs until well coated. Sprinkle over contents of casserole. Bake for 15 to 20 minutes at 350 degrees or until bread crumbs are browned and sauce is bubbly.

Yield: 4 servings

STUFFED SHAD PRESQU'ILE

3 pounds fresh, washed spinach

6 quarts boiling salted water

4 tablespoons butter

1-1/2 tablespoons flour

1 cup light cream (heavy, if you are feeling indulgent)

Salt and pepper

2 tablespoons lemon juice

1 pound fresh mushrooms, washed, dried, and finely chopped

6 scallions or 2 shallots, minced

3 boned shad fillets, about 3/4 pound each, cut in half

White wine or vermouth

Lucky the fisherman who brings home a fresh catch of Chesapeake shad, to be made into this elegant entree.

Remove heavy stems from spinach and boil slowly in salted water for 5 minutes. Drain carefully; press and squeeze out all water. Puree the spinach in a food processor. Return it to a pan in which you have melted 2 tablespoons butter and toss until it is dry.

Sprinkle on the flour and cook briefly. Add the cream slowly, cooking until it is incorporated into a smooth puree. (You may not need all the cream.) Season with salt and pepper. Add the lemon juice, a little at a time, until it reaches a flavor you like.

A handful at a time, squeeze the chopped mushrooms in the corner of a towel to remove excess juice. Melt 2 tablespoons butter in a large skillet, and add the minced scallions or shallots. Add the chopped mushrooms and toss until browned and all water has evaporated. Season with salt and pepper and fold into spinach mixture.

Butter a shallow glass or enameled baking dish. Place 3 fish halves in dish, skin-side down. Spoon stuffing on top of each half. Place the remaining 3 halves on top of the stuffing, skin-side up, and tuck them neatly to make three rectangles. (You may not need to use all the stuffing.)

Dot fish with butter and pour white wine or vermouth around fish to depth of 1/4 inch. Bake in preheated 350-degree oven for 25 to 30 minutes, basting frequently with the wine and butter.

Stuffing can be prepared in advance and refrigerated. Bring to room temperature and stuff fish just before baking.

Yield: 6 servings

BLUEFISH BAYBURY

Even the staunchest "I don't like bluefish" protestors will become converts if you remove the dark meat and soak fillets in milk before cooking.

1 fresh bluefish fillet

2 tablespoons butter, softened

1/8 teaspoon *each* dried thyme, rosemary, oregano, basil, marjoram, and sage

1 teaspoon minced green onion

Teriyaki sauce

2 slices of lemon

Lay bluefish fillet on the center of a large square of aluminum foil. Mix butter, herbs, and onion together. Spread on top of fillet. Shake on enough teriyaki sauce to have a "run-off" on the foil. Place lemon slices on top of fillet.

Cover fillet with the rest of foil. Place on a barbeque grill or in a 350-degree oven for 15 to 20 minutes. Fish will "flake" easily when tested with a fork when it is done.

Yield: 2 servings

SAUTEED FISH WITH PECAN SAUCE

Pop four baking potatoes into the microwave, and dinner will be ready in 10 minutes.

Fresh fish fillets for 4, cut into serving pieces

Flour seasoned with salt and pepper

2 tablespoons butter or margarine

1/4 cup dry white wine

Juice of 1/2 lemon

1 teaspoon Worcestershire sauce

1/2 cup chopped pecans

2 scallions, chopped, including tops

Dip fillets in seasoned flour. Shake off excess flour. Heat butter or margarine in a skillet.

Sauté fish until done, turning once to lightly brown both sides. Remove from pan and place on a platter.

Add wine, lemon juice, Worcestershire sauce, pecans, and scallions to pan. Bring to a boil. Stir and boil 1 minute. Pour over fish fillets and serve.

Yield: 4 servings

FIELD
AND
COVE

HINTS FOR COOKING WILDFOWL

Clean immediately; soak overnight in salted water to extract blood; drain.

Contrary to popular belief, goose is not greasy and in fact, like duck, should not be overcooked.

To prevent dryness, the best methods of cooking fowl are by roasting in a bag with some water, roasting in a clay pot, or roasting in a bacon wrapping.

Marinades disguise truly wild flavors (for better or worse, depending on personal preference).

Wildfowl are better served medium, not well done.

Add a whole potato, celery stalks, a quartered onion or apple to cavity or cooking vessel to remove some of the gamey flavor.

Classic accompaniments for wildfowl and game include cabbage or sauerkraut, currant jelly, turnips and turnip greens, pureed parsnips, chestnuts, mushrooms, brandied fruits, and creamed celery.

FOOLPROOF GOOSE

Beginners need no luck with this guaranteed method of preparing succulent wildfowl.

1 teaspoon garlic powder

1-1/2 cups red wine

1 large onion, quartered

1 apple, quartered

1 orange, quartered

1 goose

SAUCE:

1 tablespoon lemon juice

1 teaspoon garlic powder

1 teaspoon cinnamon

1 cup peach jam

1/4 cup of wine marinade

Mix red wine and garlic powder together. Pour over onion, apple, and orange, and soak while preparing goose.

To prepare goose, cut off loose fat, pull off excess quills. Wash well and pat dry. Prick skin with fork, and salt and pepper cavity. Put goose in plastic bag large enough to cover goose and twist shut. Fill cavity with apple, orange, onion, and wine solution. Fasten bag.

The goose can now sit at room temperature for up to 4 hours before cooking or can be prepared the day before, to this point, and refrigerated. Rotate the bag often to completely marinate the goose.

Remove goose from bag. Place on rack in roasting pan. Pour some of the wine marinade from the bag into the cavity (reserve 1/4 cup marinade for sauce). Roast for 1 hour at 375 degrees, basting occasionally with the marinade.

To make sauce, combine all ingredients and boil for 5 minutes. Cook goose an additional 1/2 hour, basting with sauce until glazed. Serve sliced goose with wild rice and remaining sauce.

Yield: 2 to 4 servings,
depending on size of goose

GOURMET GOOSE·————————————————

1 cup red wine

2 tablespoons soy sauce

2 tablespoons teriyaki sauce

1/2 teaspoon garlic powder

1 teaspoon onion salt

1 tablespoon Worcestershire sauce

1/4 teaspoon pepper

2 Canada goose breasts, skinned

This recipe was created to increase the appeal of goose to young children. It also makes an outstanding hors d'oeuvre.

Mix marinade ingredients together in large bowl. Add goose breasts and marinate for 6 to 8 hours, turning breasts often, in the refrigerator.

Cook over charcoal fire as you would steak, approximately 15 minutes. Serve as an entree, or cut into bite-size pieces and serve with toothpicks as a unique appetizer.

Yield: 4 entree servings

Roast Breast Of Goose

*Bourbon, bacon, and a bird . . .
stuffed with savory sausage*

1 young goose
1/2-pound pork sausage
Sage, oregano and tarragon (*or* poultry seasoning)
2 to 3 slices bacon
1/2 cup water
1/2 cup bourbon whiskey *or* 1/2 cup orange juice

Remove breasts from young goose and then remove skin from breasts. Place 1 breast skinned-side down, and cover with a layer of pork sausage about 1/2 inch thick. Sprinkle with sage, oregano and tarragon *or* poultry seasoning.

Place second breast on top of sausage, skinned-side up. Tie the two breasts together 4 or 5 times with string. Place slices of bacon on top of roast lengthwise.

Put roast in pan with water and bourbon whiskey *or* orange juice. Place pan in preheated oven at 350 degrees. Depending on size of breasts, roast for about 45 minutes to 1 hour, basting several times and adding more liquid, if necessary.

Remove roast from oven and let stand 5 to 10 minutes before carving. Add cooked chopped goose liver to liquid in pan for gravy.

Yield: 2 servings

Clay Pot Goose

*Cooking wildfowl in a clay pot,
essentially a steaming method,
requires less time than roasting
and results in moister, more
tender meat.*

1 whole goose, cleaned
1 16-ounce can sauerkraut, drained (reserve juice)
Salt and pepper to taste

Soak the clay pot and lid in water 10 to 15 minutes. Place juice from drained sauerkraut in bottom of pot. Stuff goose cavity with sauerkraut.

Place goose breast-side down in pot. Season to taste. Cover and bake at 350 degrees for 1 to 1-1/4 hours. Discard sauerkraut.

Yield: 4 servings

ROAST CANADA GOOSE

One Canada goose (fully thawed if taken from freezer)
2 oranges
1 6-ounce can frozen orange juice concentrate

Pungent with the flavor and aroma of fresh oranges.

Thoroughly clean and dry goose, inside and out, Be sure to remove all fat around cavity opening. Lightly salt body cavity.

Cut up 2 oranges into small sections, skin and all. Insert half of the cut-up oranges in front of cavity. Add half the orange juice concentrate in the center of the cavity. Stuff remainder of oranges in back of cavity and loosely close cavity opening.

Line bottom of roasting pan with foil and place goose in pan, uncovered. Roast in 375-degree preheated oven for not over 2 hours. Baste occasionally with other half of orange juice concentrate.

Spit Roasting: Follow preparation instructions above. Goose should baste itself. As the body cavity is somewhat loosely closed, the orange juice will leak out and roll around the rotating bird.

For a tasty accompanying sauce, heat a 10-ounce jar of currant jelly in a saucepan, and thin with red wine to a slightly thickened consistency. While sauce is cooking, grate 1 tablespoon of orange peel into it. Serve hot and pass separately.

Yield: 1 goose

BARBEQUED GOOSE BREAST

Throw another bird on the barbie!

1 whole goose breast, boned, skinned, and split
Meat tenderizer
Lemon pepper
Garlic powder
1 cup Italian salad dressing
2 tablespoons Worcestershire sauce
1/8 cup red wine vinegar

Prick goose breasts with a fork. Sprinkle meat tenderizer, lemon pepper, and garlic powder over breasts. Set aside for 15 to 20 minutes for flavors to absorb.

In shallow dish, mix salad dressing, Worcestershire sauce, and red wine vinegar. (**Note:** Marinade should be about 3/4 inches deep in dish; add additional ingredients to taste, if necessary.) Marinate goose breasts in refrigerator 4 hours; turn occasionally.

Barbeque breasts on high heat approximately 8 minutes per side, basting occasionally with marinade. Breasts should not be overcooked. Tenderness of the breasts is increased if meat is sliced on the crossgrain, as for London Broil.

Yield: 4 servings

HOW TO COOK YOUR GOOSE

Hang in a cool place for three days before plucking, gutting and freezing or eating.

Thaw, if frozen, wash and dry. Sprinkle salt and celery seed in cavity.

Stuff cavity with a quartered onion, a quartered apple, two stalks of celery, plus a few sausages at the end. Pour in 2 tablespoons brandy.

Rub butter or margarine on breast and legs. Sprinkle with celery seed, salt, pepper and sesame seed. Lay strips of butter over breast. Sprinkle with paprika and put in roasting pan with cored apple halves.

Preheat oven to 500 degrees. Cook goose at this temperature for 5 minutes to seal in the juices. Reduce temperature to 350 degrees and cook for 30 to 40 minutes, depending on the size of the goose.

Place on a platter with apples and sausages around it. Make longitudinal cuts of breast, 1/2 inch wide.

Yield: 1 goose

HOW TO FOIL YOUR DUCK

1 wild duck
Salt
1 medium apple
1 medium onion
1 stalk celery
1 tablespoon butter
1/4 cup honey
1/4 cup orange juice
1 teaspoon grated orange peel
1/4 teaspoon ground ginger
1/4 teaspoon dried basil

Salt duck, inside and out. Stuff with apple, onion and celery. Place duck on a large piece of heavy aluminum foil.

Melt butter and combine with remaining ingredients. Pour half the sauce inside the duck and half over the top. Fold foil tightly around bird.

Bake in preheated 425-degree oven for 1 hour and 45 minutes. Open foil and return to oven for 15 to 20 minutes to brown. (To foil a goose, increase sauce ingredients by one half and bake for 2 hours and 15 minutes before opening foil.)

Yield: 1 duck

TWICE BAGGED BIRD

If you have never cooked wildfowl in a roasting bag, this technique will be a happy surprise.

Duck or other wildfowl, cleaned
2 tablespoons salt
Water
Salt and pepper to taste
1 cooking bag
1 tablespoon chopped onions
1/2 cup water
Carrots and potatoes

12 hours in advance of cooking or freezing: If a freshly-bagged bird is being prepared, in a large container combine salt with enough water to cover. Soak overnight to remove blood. Rinse with cold water and drain. (If this step is omitted, blood clots will remain in the meat, and the bird will have a wilder, more gamey flavor.)

Season bird with salt and pepper and place in cooking bag. Scatter onion inside cavity and around outside of bird. Add water to cooking bag. Peel carrots and potatoes and cut into large pieces. Place around bird in bag. Place bag in roasting pan.

Seal bag. Puncture with 6 small holes. Roast at 350 degrees for 2 to 2-1/2 hours, until meat falls away from breastbone.

Yield: 1 bird

DUCK BREAST IN TAWNY PORT

Elegant, yet easy to prepare.

4 duck breast halves, boned and skinned (save one piece of skin)
1 cup tawny port
2 cups rich duck, veal or beef stock, unsalted and degreased
1/2 teaspoon salt
1/8 teaspoon pepper

Trim all fat, tendons and "silver skin" off duck breasts.

In a medium saucepan, bring port to a boil and reduce over high heat to 1/4 cup. Add stock and continue to boil rapidly until liquid is reduced to 3/4 cup. Keep warm, or reheat when ready to serve.

In a skillet large enough to hold the duck breasts in one layer without crowding, put the reserved piece of duck skin. Heat until about 2 tablespoons of fat are rendered (1 to 2 minutes). Remove skin. Season duck breasts with salt and pepper. Sauté in duck fat until browned on each side—3 to 4 minutes total—so the meat is still medium rare.

Remove from skillet and let sit in a warm oven on a plate for 5 minutes. Drain juices from warming plate into the sauce. Reheat sauce. Slice each breast into about 5 vertical slices. Fan out on a pool of sauce on warmed plates. Brush slices with a bit of sauce to glaze. Serve hot.

Yield: 4 servings

SMOKED BLUEFISH

Bluefish fillets
Teriyaki sauce
Olive oil
Lemon pepper

Big blues are best—5 pounds or more! Or look for the largest fillets you can buy.

Lay fillets skin-side down. Sprinkle with teriyaki sauce; rub lightly with olive oil, and dust with lemon pepper.

Prepare smoker with coals, adding a handful of mesquite chips to float in the water pan. Also have ready a pail of mesquite chips soaking in water.

Lay fillets skin-side down on grill. Cook for approximately 2-1/2 hours, adjusting temperature and cooking time as needed. (This is an art, not a science—be prepared to experiment!) Toss a handful of pre-soaked mesquite chips directly onto the coals every 45 minutes. Test fish by pressing with your thumb or a plastic spoon. Fillets will feel firm with a slight "give" when done. Don't overcook.

Serve with raspberry or cherry sauce for an entree, or cool and spear bite-size pieces with toothpicks for hors d'oeuvres.

TIPSY RAISIN STUFFING

Sherry-soaked raisins highlight this delicious dressing.

1/4 pound butter
1 10-ounce can chicken stock
1 clove garlic, minced
4 ounces white wine
8 ounces herb-seasoned stuffing crumbs
8 ounces stuffing cubes
2 cups chopped celery
2 cups chopped onion
2 cups chopped Granny Smith apples, unpeeled
8 ounces chopped English walnuts (do not use black walnuts)
1 cup chopped fresh parsley
2 teaspoons fresh ground nutmeg
2 teaspoons cinnamon
1 teaspoon fresh ground pepper
8 ounces sherry (your favorite type)
1 cup raisins

In a small saucepan, combine butter, stock, garlic and wine. Heat to melt butter. Remove from heat.

In a large bowl, thoroughly mix crumbs and cubes, celery, onion, apples, nuts, parsley, and seasonings.

In a small saucepan, heat sherry and raisins. Stir frequently until all sherry is absorbed. Add raisins to stuffing mixture. Pour in stock and mix thoroughly. Loosely stuff a 12- to 14-pound bird.

Place remaining stuffing in a baking dish. Cover with foil, poking a few holes. Bake at 375 degrees for 40 to 50 minutes.

Yield: Dressing for 12 to 14 pounds of fowl

Wild Rice Casserole

1/2 cup chopped onion
1 cup sliced mushrooms
1/4 cup salad oil
8 ounces wild rice
1 cup shredded cheese
1 cup sliced ripe olives (optional)
1 cup canned tomatoes
1 can tomato soup

Sauté onions and mushrooms in salad oil until tender.

Cook wild rice in boiling water to cover, plus 1 inch, for 50 to 60 minutes.

Combine all ingredients and simmer until they are well blended, or bake in the oven at 350 degrees for 1/2 hour.

Can be prepared a day ahead.   Yield: 4 servings

Wild rice and mushrooms . . . the ideal accompaniment to wild game.

Currant Sauce

1 small onion, minced
1 tablespoon butter or margarine
2 tablespoons cornstarch
1 cup chicken broth or beef bouillon
Grated peel of one orange
1 12-ounce jar currant jelly.

Brown onion in butter or margarine.

Stir in remaining ingredients and cook until thick and glossy. Let stand 12 hours.

Rewarm over low heat. Serve with chicken or wildfowl.

Prepare in advance.   Yield: 3 cups

Excellent accompaniment for all fowl.

CRANBERRY CHUTNEY

Cranberry sauce with a spicy flair, to enhance all fowl or your favorite roast.

1 orange, thinly sliced, including peel
1/2 lemon, thinly sliced, including peel
1/2 cup water
1/2 cup brown sugar
1 pound fresh cranberries
1 tart apple, pared, cored, and coarsely grated
1-1/2 cups brown sugar
3/4 cup vinegar
1/2 cup raisins
1/2 teaspoon salt
1/2 teaspoon dry mustard
1/4 teaspoon ginger
1/4 teaspoon cloves
1/4 teaspoon allspice
2 teaspoons chili powder

Cook orange and lemon in 1/2 cup water until tender. Add 1/2 cup brown sugar and cook until slightly thickened.

Combine remaining ingredients with fruit mixture and bring to a boil. Reduce heat and simmer, uncovered, 15 minutes, stirring often. Pour into jars while hot and seal.

Serve with chicken or wildfowl.

Yield: 5 to 6 8-ounce jars

GARDEN PATCH

Harvest Slaw

Pineapple flavors both salad and dressing in this colorful slaw.

1/2 head large cabbage, shredded

2 red apples, unpeeled, diced

2 stalks celery, diced

2 cups raisins

1 10-ounce can crushed pineapple, drained with juice reserved

2 cups mayonnaise *or* salad dressing ♥

2 teaspoons sugar

2 teaspoons vinegar

1 teaspoon prepared mustard

1/4 teaspoon each ground pepper and celery salt

Mix together cabbage, apples, celery, raisins, and drained pineapple.

Combine remaining ingredients, including reserved pineapple juice, to make dressing. Toss with slaw mixture and refrigerate several hours before serving.

Prepare in advance.   Yield: 8 servings

Classic Potato Salad

Grandma's favorite boiled dressing reappears in this modern version.

7 medium potatoes, peeled

3 ribs celery, chopped

1 small onion, chopped

4 slices bacon, cooked and crumbled

Boiled dressing:

1/2 cup sugar

1 teaspoon salt

1 teaspoon dry mustard

2 tablespoons flour

2 eggs, well beaten

1/2 cup vinegar

1/2 cup water

2 tablespoons butter or margarine

Cook potatoes and cut into bite-size pieces. Add celery, onion, and bacon. Combine with enough boiled dressing to moisten.

To prepare boiled dressing, blend dry ingredients into beaten eggs. Heat vinegar and water; add egg mixture and cook until thick. Beat in butter and allow to cool.

Note: The boiled dressing can also be used for chicken salad.

Yield: 4 to 6 servings

Sweet Potato Salad

4 pounds sweet potatoes, peeled and cubed
1 20-ounce can pineapple chunks (unsweetened), drained
5 ribs celery, chopped
1 cup walnuts, chopped
1 cup raisins

DRESSING:
1 cup mayonnaise
1-1/2 cups dairy sour cream
1 tablespoon brown sugar
1 teaspoon salt
1 teaspoon grated ginger root
1/2 teaspoon nutmeg
1/2 teaspoon cloves
1/2 teaspoon cinnamon
Grated zest of 1 lemon
Grated zest of 1 orange

Surprise your family with this delicious "new" version of potato salad.

Boil sweet potatoes until tender (about 12 minutes). Drain and rinse with cool water. When potatoes are dry, combine with pineapple, celery, walnuts, and raisins in a large mixing bowl.

In a separate mixing bowl, combine dressing ingredients; toss gently with potato mixture. Best when flavors have been allowed to blend overnight.

Prepare in advance.

Yield: 10 to 12 servings

SUMMER VEGETABLE SALAD

Tasty any time of the year, but especially delicious in the summer with fresh Eastern Shore vegetables.

2 cups sliced green beans, cooked crisp
2 cups white corn, cooked
1 cup chopped celery
3/4 cup chopped onion
1/2 cup chopped green pepper
1 teaspoon chopped parsley
1 2-ounce jar pimento, chopped
1 small tomato, diced (optional)

DRESSING:
3/4 cup wine vinegar
1/2 cup salad oil
3/4 cup sugar
Salt and pepper to taste

Mix all ingredients together. Stir well and refrigerate overnight, or at least 8 hours.

Note: Canned or frozen vegetables may be used if fresh are not available.

Prepare in advance.   Yield: 8 to 10 servings

SPINACH SALAD DUO

Apples and bleu cheese add a colorful twist to this spinach salad with a choice of dressings.

1 pound fresh spinach, rinsed and well dried
2 small apples, unpeeled, diced
6 strips bacon, fried crisp and crumbled
3/4 cup crumbled bleu cheese
1/2 cup broken walnuts
1/2 cup sour cream
1 cup mayonnaise
1/2 teaspoon salt
1/8 teaspoon coarse ground pepper

Remove tough stems from spinach and tear into bite-size pieces. Toss with apple bits, bacon, 1/2 cup crumbled bleu cheese, and walnuts.

Combine remaining 1/4 cup bleu cheese with sour cream, mayonnaise, salt and pepper. Toss dressing with salad and serve.

Or, for a lighter dressing, substitute 1/4 cup milk and 1 tablespoon honey for the mayonnaise.

Yield: 6 to 8 servings

BROCCOLI-MUSHROOM· MARINADE

1 bunch fresh broccoli, cut into small pieces
1/2 pound fresh mushrooms, sliced
1 bunch scallions, chopped

DRESSING:
1 cup sugar
2 teaspoons paprika
1-1/2 teaspoons salt
1 cup salad oil ♥
4 tablespoons grated onion
1/2 cup vinegar
2 teaspoons celery seed

Crunchy and colorful.

Combine dressing with vegetables and marinate all day in refrigerator.

Drain well before serving.

Prepare in advance.

Yield: 4 to 6 servings

RECIPE FOR SALAD DRESSING

This circa 1890 salad dressing recipe from the galley of the steamer, Fish Hawk, was found amongst the private memorabilia and papers of St. Michaels businessman, Thomas Sewell. Mr. Sewell was the proprietor of a local drug store and print shop whose establishment also served as the library. An avid photographer, many of his images appeared on postcards which he sold in his shop.

Tested by Chesapeake Bay Maritime Museum employees, this Victorian era salad dressing was pronounced excellent. (Note: research indicated the sweet oil called for in the recipe is olive oil.)

1/2 teaspoonful Coleman's Mustard
1 tablespoonful pulverized sugar
1/2 teaspoonful of salt
The yolk of an egg

Mix dry mustard, salt and sugar together, and when smooth, mix yolk of egg in. Mix together for five minutes, then drop sweet oil in gradually until it becomes thick; then work in about 1/2 pint sweet oil, and thin down with juice of half a lemon, then put in vinegar to suit the taste. If mixed as directed, it will be correct. This is enough dressing for six.

J. G. Thompson, Steward

ITALIAN WINE DRESSING

Choose a good quality, dry red wine for this versatile dressing.

1/3 cup red wine
1/3 cup red wine vinegar
1/3 cup catsup
3/4 cup olive oil
1 teaspoon Worcestershire sauce
1/2 teaspoon dry mustard
1 teaspoon sugar
1/4 teaspoon salt
1/8 teaspoon coarsely ground pepper
1 large clove garlic, minced

Put all ingredients together in a pint jar and shake well. Refrigerate until ready to use. Olive oil solidifies in the refrigerator, so remove jar about 1 hour before serving and shake well.

Yield: 2 cups

Spinach Maria

3 tablespoons oil

1 medium onion, chopped

1 10-ounce box frozen chopped spinach, thawed and drained

2 to 3 slices white bread, crumbled

2 tablespoons grated Parmesan cheese

"Another way to prepare spinach," says the author—and a delicious one!

In a 10-inch frying pan, heat oil and sauté chopped onion until golden. Remove from heat.

Add thawed spinach, crumbled white bread, and grated Parmesan cheese. Mix well. Return to low burner and cook, covered, for 5 minutes.

Yield: 4 servings

Cheesy Cabbage

3 cups shredded cabbage

1 quart boiling water

3 tablespoons butter or margarine

3 tablespoons flour

Salt and pepper to taste

1-1/2 cups milk

3/4 cup shredded Swiss or Cheddar cheese

1/2 cup seasoned bread crumbs, mixed with 2 tablespoons melted butter

Vary this interesting blend of flavors by choosing different cheeses—perhaps shredded Parmesan or dilled Havarti.

In a medium saucepan, cook cabbage for 15 minutes in boiling water. Drain well.

Meanwhile, melt butter in small saucepan. Add flour and seasonings and stir for 1 minute. Add milk and stir until well blended and thickened.

Alternate layers of cabbage, shredded cheese and warm sauce in a 9-inch glass pie pan. Top with buttered crumbs. Bake at 350 degrees for 20 minutes, or until nicely browned.

Yield: 6 servings

BAKED ASPARAGUS DIJON

Fresh asparagus comes shining through a deftly flavored cream sauce.

2 pounds fresh asparagus, washed, tough ends removed
1 cup light cream
1/2 pound fresh mushrooms, sliced thin
1 teaspoon sugar
Salt and pepper to taste
1 cup shredded Monterey jack cheese
1 teaspoon lemon juice
1 teaspoon Dijon mustard
3 hard-cooked eggs, finely chopped
1/2 cup bread crumbs

Slice asparagus on the diagonal into 1-1/2-inch pieces. Plunge into a kettle of boiling water and cook 3 to 4 minutes, until barely tender. Drain immediately. Place in 2-quart casserole.

In medium saucepan, heat cream to simmering. Add mushrooms, sugar, salt and pepper. Simmer for 5 minutes (don't boil). Remove from heat and add shredded cheese, lemon juice and mustard. Stir until cheese melts.

Pour mushroom sauce over asparagus pieces. Sprinkle on chopped eggs and bread crumbs. Bake at 350 degrees for 25 to 30 minutes, until heated through.

Yield: 4 servings

SILVER QUEEN SOUFFLE

Our succulent Silver Queen corn becomes a mid-summer staple on supper tables. Here is a Sunday-dinner special way to enjoy it.

2 tablespoons butter or margarine♥
2 tablespoons flour
1-1/2 teaspoons salt
1/8 teaspoon pepper
1 cup milk♥
2 cups fresh corn, scraped from cob
2 eggs, separated♥

Melt butter in large saucepan. Blend in flour, salt and pepper. Gradually stir in milk and cook over low heat, stirring constantly, until thick. Add corn and mix well.

Beat egg whites until stiff and set aside. Beat egg yolks until thick and lemon-colored, and stir into corn mixture. Fold in egg whites and pour into buttered 1-1/2 quart casserole.

Bake in preheated oven at 350 degrees for 30 minutes. Serve immediately.

Low-cholesterol conversion:
Substitute margarine for butter and skim milk for whole milk. Instead of 2 eggs, use 2 egg substitutes instead of egg yolks. Use two egg whites, kept separate from egg substitutes, beaten stiff.

Yield: 4 to 6 servings

Lout's Sprouts

1-1/4 pounds Brussels sprouts

2 cups water

4 slices bacon, diced

4 tablespoons bacon drippings

1 medium onion, finely chopped

3/4 teaspoon dry mustard

3/4 teaspoon caraway seed

1-1/2 teaspoons brown sugar

1/4 cup red wine vinegar

1 cup sweet red pepper, coarsely chopped

Chopped parsley

A crisp, colorful vegetable with a delightful sweet and sour taste. This dish will tempt even the most skeptical of vegetable eaters.

Rinse Brussels sprouts and remove damaged leaves. Score root end of each sprout. In a saucepan bring water to a boil; add cleaned sprouts and simmer 5 to 7 minutes until tender but still crisp. Drain and plunge into cold water; drain and dry on paper towels. Cut each sprout in half lengthwise.

In a large skillet over medium heat, fry diced bacon; remove to paper towel when lightly browned. Remove all but 4 tablespoons of drippings from the pan. Add onion and sauté until tender. Stir in dry mustard, caraway seeds, brown sugar, and red wine vinegar. Bring to a boil. Add Brussels sprouts and red pepper; sauté only long enough to reheat the Brussels sprouts.

Set aside 1 tablespoon bacon. Toss remaining bacon with sprouts and peppers; remove to a warm serving bowl. Sprinkle with remaining bacon and chopped parsley, if desired.

Yield: 4 to 6 servings

ZESTY WINTER CARROTS

Life-long carrot-haters have been converted by this flavorful combination. We guarantee it!

2 tablespoons chopped onion
2 tablespoons butter or margarine
1-1/2 pounds raw carrots, peeled
1/2 cup mayonnaise or salad dressing ♥
2 tablespoons horseradish
Salt and pepper to taste
1/4 cup bread crumbs mixed with 1 tablespoon melted butter or margarine

Sauté onions in butter or margarine until limp.

Using a food processor, *coarsely* shred or *thinly* slice the carrots. Add to onion and cook over medium heat, stirring frequently, for 5 minutes. Mix in mayonnaise, horseradish and seasoning.

Place mixture in 1-1/2-quart casserole and sprinkle with buttered bread crumbs. Bake at 350 degrees for 25 to 30 minutes.

Yield: 6 servings

TWICE-BAKED SWEET POTATOES

A familiar technique with a spicy, sweet twist.

2 medium sweet potatoes
1 tablespoon maple syrup
1 tablespoon butter or margarine
Dash cinnamon
Dash ginger
2 tablespoons chopped pecans

Scrub potatoes and bake at 375 degrees for 40 to 45 minutes, until tender. Cut a small lengthwise slice from the top of each potato. Scoop out potato into mixing bowl, leaving 1/2-inch shells.

Add maple syrup, butter, cinnamon, and ginger to potatoes and mash. Stir in 1 tablespoon pecans. Spoon mixture into shells.

Place in shallow baking dish. (Cover and chill, if making ahead.) Top potatoes with remaining pecans and drizzle with additional maple syrup. Bake uncovered in 375-degree oven for 25 minutes, *or* microwave at 100% power (high) for 8 minutes.

Yield: 2 servings

LAYERED ZUCCHINI·

1 teaspoon butter or margarine

1 pound small zucchini, unpeeled; slice 1/4-inch thick
    lengthwise

2 small tomatoes, sliced very thin

1/2 Spanish onion, sliced very thin

Salt and pepper to taste

4 tablespoons brown sugar

4 tablespoons butter or margarine

4 tablespoons buttered bread crumbs *or* grated Parmesan
    cheese

The traditional Eastern Shore combination of brown sugar and tomatoes enlivens this squash casserole.

Spread 1 teaspoon butter or margarine around 5- by 9-inch loaf pan. Place half the zucchini slices in pan, overlapping. Cover with half the sliced tomatoes, then half the sliced onion. Sprinkle on salt and pepper to taste. Repeat layers.

Dot brown sugar and butter or margarine over top layer. Sprinkle on bread crumbs or grated cheese. Bake in 350-degree oven for 1 hour.

Yield: 4 servings

Eastern Shore Tomato Casserole

Summer on the Eastern Shore brings a boundless supply of juicy, fresh tomatoes, often prepared as a tasty vegetable casserole.

4 slices bacon

1 small onion, chopped

1-1/2 pounds fresh tomatoes (1 pound, 12-ounce can tomatoes may be substituted)

4 to 5 slices firm, white bread, cubed

1/2 cup brown sugar

1/2 teaspoon tarragon

1/2 teaspoon basil

1/4 teaspoon garlic powder (optional)

Salt and pepper to taste

Parmesan cheese

Fry bacon and drain. Sauté chopped onion in bacon fat until limp.

Chop tomatoes and place in 1-1/2-quart casserole. Stir in bread cubes, onion, brown sugar, and spices.

Bake at 350 degrees for 20 minutes. Sprinkle with Parmesan cheese and crumbled bacon and bake for 10 minutes more.

Yield: 4 servings

Corn on the Cob— Little Choptank Style

Swim all day at your favorite little sand beach without benefit of lunch from home. About 4 p.m. walk up a hot, dusty farm lane with your hair still wet and sweat tricklin' down your back and walk into a field of tall, green corn.

Pull off about half a dozen freshly matured ears (you can tell because only the tips of the silk have started to wither) and carry them to a place where you can sit and husk the ears and bite into the sun-warmed, golden, juicy kernels for the sweetest eating since last year.

Brunch to Lunch

SOUTHERN MARYLAND STUFFED HAM

A southern Maryland specialty, a whole country ham is stuffed and precooked. Then it is refrigerated for at least 12 hours, carved in paper-thin slices, and served cold. Stuffed ham is traditionally served as either a first course or as an accompaniment to roast chicken or other fowl.

18 to 20-pound ham
2 parts kale
1 part cabbage
1 bunch celery
2 large onions, chopped
2 to 3 tablespoons red pepper flakes
2 to 3 tablespoons mustard seed
Mustard

Chop and blanch vegetables until limp; drain and reserve liquid. Mix vegetables with mustard. Cut incisions in ham lengthwise. Stuff slits with vegetable mixture. Pile leftover mix on top of ham, wrap in cheesecloth and fasten.

Put on rack in pot, cover with leftover liquid and water to cover. Cover and simmer about four hours. Refrigerate overnight before slicing.

If using pre-cooked ham, 2 to 3 hours simmering time.

BAKED BREAKFAST GENESIS

Something fancy for Sunday breakfast or brunch on board.

1/4 cup butter, softened
6 slices bread, trimmed
6 slices Gouda cheese, *or* **10-ounce ball Edam, sliced**
2 eggs
1 cup milk
Salt and pepper to taste
Dash of nutmeg

Butter a 1-quart baking dish or 8- × 8-inch square pan. Also, butter bread on 1 side. Arrange bread in pan, buttered side up. Overlap slices, if necessary. Top with cheese slices.

Beat eggs with milk and add salt, pepper, and nutmeg. Pour over bread and cheese. Bake at 350 degrees for 30 to 40 minutes, or until golden and puffed. Serve with sausages and fresh mixed fruit.

Yield: 4 to 6 servings

CRUNCHY BRUNCH SOUFFLE

16 slices good-quality white bread

6 eggs

3 cups milk

1/2 teaspoon onion salt

1/2 teaspoon dry mustard

12 ounces Swiss cheese, grated

12 ounces Cheddar cheese, grated

16 ounces thinly-sliced baked or deli ham

3 cups corn flakes

1/2 cup melted butter

Ham and eggs dress up Sunday-special in this attractive casserole dish.

Remove crust and cut bread slices in half.

Whisk together eggs, milk, onion salt and dry mustard.

In a greased 9- × 13-inch pan, layer half the bread, half the cheeses and half the ham; repeat. Pour egg mixture over layers and cover; refrigerate overnight. (May be frozen at this point.)

Sprinkle corn flakes over casserole and drizzle with melted butter. Bake for 40 minutes at 375 degrees.

Yield: 10 to 12 servings

SANDWICH AT EASE

1 large flour tortilla

4 slices imported Swiss cheese

2 slices prosciutto

1 scallion or 1 thin stalk asparagus

3 heaping tablespoons lump crabmeat, moistened with mayonnaise

Butter

Great for boat food—quick, easy, and no mess. Slice into bite-size pieces for hors d'oeuvres.

Lay tortilla on cookie sheet and place the following in center of tortilla: cheese, ham, scallion or asparagus, and crabmeat. Fold one side firmly over the other and lay fold side down. Lightly butter top.

Heat oven to 400 degrees and bake tortilla for 5 to 7 minutes until top is brown. Slice in half and serve warm.

Yield: 2 servings

SPINACH PINWHEEL

Serve with steaming bowls of minestrone or chowder for a hearty supper, or sliced into thirds for a hot hors d'oeuvre.

ITALIAN BREAD DOUGH:
1 package dry yeast
1/4 cup warm water (105 to 115 degrees) with a splash of olive oil
3 cups flour (preferably unbleached)
1/2 teaspoon baking powder
1 teaspoon salt
1/2 cup warm milk
1/2 cup warm water

SPINACH FILLING:
2 10-ounce packages frozen chopped spinach, thawed and drained
3 tablespoons olive oil
1 small clove garlic, minced
1/2 teaspoon crushed red pepper
1/2 teaspoon oregano
2 eggs
1/4 cup grated Romano cheese
1 cup shredded mozzarella cheese
2 2-ounce cans anchovy fillets, drained (optional)

Dissolve yeast in 1/4 cup warm water.

Combine flour, baking powder and salt in a large bowl, and make a well in the center. Pour yeast mixture, warm milk and water into well. Mix until dough forms a ball.

Knead dough until soft and springy, adding more flour as needed. Return dough to a lightly oiled bowl. Cover with a clean towel and set in a warm place to rise, about 1-1/2 hours. Punch down and let rest 10 minutes, while you prepare filling.

In a large skillet, combine spinach, 2 tablespoons olive oil, garlic, red pepper and oregano. Sauté, stirring frequently, for 4 or 5 minutes. Remove from heat.

Into spinach mixture, stir 1 whole egg plus 1 egg white (reserve yolk). Mix in grated Romano cheese.

On a floured board, roll out dough into an 11- × 18-inch rectangle. Rub surface with 1 tablespoon olive oil. Spread spinach mixture over dough and sprinkle with grated mozzarella cheese. Lay anchovy fillets on cheese, if desired.

Fold in ends of dough and roll up, jelly-roll style. Place loaf on lightly oiled baking sheet and brush with beaten egg yolk. Bake at 350 degrees for 45 minutes or until golden brown.

Yield: 8 to 10 servings

TROPICAL FRENCH TOAST

1 1-pound loaf French bread *or* thick-sliced firm white sandwich bread

1 cup orange juice

1/2 cup milk

2 large eggs

2 tablespoons sugar

1 teaspoon ground cinnamon

1/8 teaspoon nutmeg

Butter or margarine

Add a splash of golden rum to your maple syrup, and you'll hear the rustle of island breezes across the breakfast table.

Several hours or the night before serving, slice French bread crosswise into inch-thick slices. Let stand until ready to use. (Let sandwich bread slices stand open for an hour or so.)

Whisk together orange juice, milk, eggs, sugar and spices. Pour into large shallow pan and add bread slices, turning several times as liquid is absorbed.

Melt 2 tablespoons butter or margarine on a large griddle. Add soaked bread and cook, turning as needed, until golden brown on both sides—about 4 minutes total. Control heat and cooking time so bread does not scorch. Continue to cook in batches, adding butter as needed.

Serve hot with warmed maple syrup.

Prepare in advance.

Yield: 4 to 6 servings

Hearty Oat Muffins

Low in cholesterol and high in fiber, these muffins combine well with any fruit you fancy. Try bananas put through the blender, or apples or pears (unpeeled) chopped in a food processor. Then there are raisins, blueberries, dates, cranberries, zucchini—you choose!

1/4 cup whole wheat flour
1 cup oat bran cereal
1 cup wheat bran
1 tablespoon baking powder
1 teaspoon cinnamon *or* nutmeg
1/4 cup brown sugar *or* honey *or* molasses
2 egg whites
2 tablespoons vegetable oil
1-1/4 cups skim milk
1 cup fruit and/or nuts

In a large bowl, combine first 5 ingredients and brown sugar, if used.

In a separate bowl, beat egg whites until foamy. Mix in honey or molasses, if used, vegetable oil, and milk. Stir to combine.

Stir egg white mixture into dry ingredients and add chopped fruits and/or nuts. Spoon into muffin tins which have been sprayed with vegetable oil spray. Bake in preheated 425-degree oven for 15 to 17 minutes, or until a toothpick inserted in center of muffin comes out moist but not wet.

Recipe can be doubled.   Yield: 12 muffins

Poppy Seed Loaf

Enjoy as a breakfast cake or dessert.

1/2 pound butter
1-1/2 cups sugar
4 eggs, separated
2-1/4 ounces poppy seeds
2-1/2 teaspoons baking powder
1/2 teaspoon salt
12 ounces dairy sour cream
2 cups flour
1-1/2 teaspoons vanilla

Cream butter and sugar. Add egg yolks and poppy seeds to the butter-sugar mixture and beat well.

Add baking powder and salt. Beat in sour cream and flour in alternating amounts.

Beat egg whites, with vanilla added, with a fork until frothy. Fold into batter. Be sure to blend well.

Pour into 2 well-greased loaf pans sprinkled with sugar. Bake at 350 degrees for 50 to 60 minutes. Top should be firm and brown.

Cool before removing from pans.

Yield: 2 loaves

FRESH PEACH COFFEE CAKE

1 egg
1 cup sugar
1/2 cup butter or margarine
2 cups sifted flour
1/2 teaspoon salt
2/3 cup milk
2 teaspoons baking powder
Fresh peaches, peeled and sliced
Cinnamon

TOPPING:
1 cup powdered sugar
1/2 teaspoon vanilla
Milk

Treat yourself to this delectable morning treat when local peaches are in season.

Beat egg until light and fluffy. Add sugar and beat until blended. Add shortening and beat until smooth.

Add sifted flour and salt to egg mixture alternately with milk, adding baking powder to last part of the flour. Batter will be stiff. (A few drops of yellow food coloring may be added, if desired.)

Spread into buttered and floured 9- × 13-inch pan. Slice enough ripe peaches to cover top of batter. Arrange in attractive design. Sprinkle generously with cinnamon. Bake at 350 degrees for 30 to 35 minutes or until cake tester comes out clean.

Mix powdered sugar with vanilla and enough milk to make a consistency that will pour off spoon. Remove cake from oven and while still warm, drizzle the icing over top.

Yield: 12 to 14 servings

ZETTA CARVER'S OATMEAL BREAD

This superb recipe was developed two generations before anyone ever heard of microwave ovens and cholesterol counts.

1 cup milk, scalded (can be done in microwave oven)♥
1/4 cup sugar
1-1/2 teaspoons salt
1/2 cup cooking oil
2 packages active dry yeast
1/4 cup warm water (105 to 115 degees)
2 eggs, slightly beaten♥
1 cup flour
2 cups old-fashioned rolled oats *or* quick-cooking oats♥
   (do not use instant oatmeal)
2-1/2 to 3 additional cups flour

Into scalded milk, stir sugar, salt and cooking oil. Cool to lukewarm.

Sprinkle yeast over warm water. Add eggs, 1 cup flour, and milk mixture to yeast in bowl. Stir in oats.

Work remaining flour into a soft dough. Turn onto a lightly floured board and knead 10 minutes or until smooth and elastic. Dough can be kneaded in a mixer with a dough hook for 7 minutes. Round dough into a ball and place smooth-side up in a well greased bowl. Turn to grease top, cover, and let rise in a warm place until double in bulk.

To let dough rise in a microwave oven, first heat 2 cups of water to boiling in a large microwave-proof container. Place the bowl of dough, uncovered, in the microwave oven with the container of water, and shut the door. The temperature will be 80 to 85 degrees, and the humidity will keep the top from drying out.

Punch dough down and turn out on floured board. Allow to rest 10 minutes. Shape into two loaves and place in greased loaf pans, turning tops as before or brushing tops with melted butter. Let rise again until nearly doubled in size.

Bake at 375 degrees about 40 minutes. For glass loaf pans, bake at 350 degrees. Turn out onto a rack to cool.

Low-cholesterol conversion:
Substitute 1 cup skim milk for whole milk. In place of eggs, use 2 egg substitutes and 1 egg white. One-half cup oat bran may be substituted for an equal amount of rolled oats. Brush tops of loaves with melted margarine instead of butter.

Yield: 2 loaves

Luscious Lemon Bread

2/3 cup melted butter

2 cups sugar

4 eggs

1/2 teaspoon almond extract

3 cups flour

2 teaspoons baking powder

1 teaspoon salt

1 cup milk

2 tablespoons grated lemon peel

Glaze:

6 tablespoons fresh lemon juice, mixed with 1/2 cup of sugar

This recipe makes two loaves, one to enjoy fresh from the oven and one to freeze and bring out as a treat on another day.

Blend melted butter and sugar. Add eggs, one at a time, beating each one in briefly. Add almond extract.

Sift flour, baking powder and salt together. Add to egg mixture alternately with the milk. Fold in the lemon peel.

Bake in 2 greased and floured loaf pans at 325 degrees for 60 to 65 minutes or until a toothpick comes out clean when inserted into center of loaf. (**Note:** if you are using glass loaf pans, bread will require from 5 to 10 minutes *less* time in baking.)

When bread is done, remove from oven and loosen bread from the sides and bottom of the pan. Immediately pour glaze over the hot bread. Cool 15 minutes, then remove bread from pans. Cool completely before freezing.

Yield: 2 loaves

ZINGY ZUCCHINI BREAD

When your zucchini threatens to take over the garden, strike back by making this wonderfully different bread. Just as good at room temperature as hot from the oven, it makes an excellent addition to a boat supper.

1/2 cup butter, softened
3/4 cup sugar
4 large eggs, beaten
1/2 cup grated extra sharp Cheddar cheese
1/2 cup grated Monterey jack cheese with jalapeno peppers
1/4 cup minced sweet onion
2 cups grated zucchini
1 cup stone-ground yellow cornmeal
1 cup white flour
4 teaspoons baking powder
1/2 teaspoon salt

In a large bowl cream together butter and sugar. Add eggs, Cheddar cheese, jack cheese, onion and zucchini, and beat well.

In a separate bowl mix cornmeal, flour, baking powder and salt. Add flour mixture to batter and mix well.

Pour into ungreased 7-1/2 × 11-1/2 × 2-inch baking pan and bake at 350 degrees for 1 hour. Cool and store in pan.

Yield: 10 to 12 servings

ORANGE SHERBET MOLD

Equally refreshing as a luncheon salad or cool dessert.

1 6-ounce package orange gelatin
2 cups boiling water
1 pint orange sherbet
2 11-ounce cans Mandarin orange slices, drained (reserve juice from half of one can)

Dissolve gelatin in boiling water. Add sherbet and stir until melted. Add orange slices and reserved juice; mix well.

Pour into a 1-quart mold, lightly sprayed with vegetable oil spray. Refrigerate several hours until firm. Unmold on lettuce for salad; garnish with orange slices for dessert.

Prepare in advance.

Yield: 12 servings

BLUEBERRY-CREAM MOLD

1 20-ounce can blueberries, drained with liquid reserved
1 20-ounce can crushed pineapple, drained with liquid reserved
1 6-ounce package black raspberry gelatin

TOPPING:
1 8-ounce package cream cheese, softened
1 pint dairy sour cream
1/2 cup sugar
1 teaspoon vanilla

The unexpected deep blue color makes this a dramatic addition to a buffet table.

In a medium saucepan, heat together reserved liquid from blueberries and pineapple. Add black raspberry gelatin and stir until dissolved. Stir in blueberries and pineapple. Pour into 8-inch square dish. Chill until firm.

Combine topping ingredients and beat until smooth. Pour over chilled gelatin and return to refrigerator for several hours.

Prepare in advance.   Yield: 9 servings

BAYLINER PEANUT SOUP

1 medium onion, chopped
2 ribs celery, chopped
1/4 cup butter
3 tablespoons flour
2 quarts chicken broth
2 cups creamy peanut butter
1-3/4 cups light cream
Chopped peanuts for garnish

This historic soup was a favorite of passengers cruising the Chesapeake on ships of the Old Bay Line.

Sauté onion and celery in butter. Press through colander. Return to kettle and add flour, then chicken broth. Bring to a boil, stirring constantly.

Stir in peanut butter until smooth. Lower heat and add cream. Blend thoroughly, but do not boil. Sprinkle chopped peanuts on each serving.

                    Yield: 12 servings

CHESSIE CORN CHOWDER

A hearty soup, enriched with the smoky aroma of bacon and the texture of corn and potatoes.

6 to 8 slices bacon, chopped

1/2 cup chopped onion

1/2 cup chopped green pepper

1/4 cup dried parsley

2 cups fresh corn, scraped from cob (1 20-ounce can cream-style corn may be substituted)

1 can cream of celery soup

3/4 cup water

3/4 cup milk

1/2 cup instant potato flakes *or* **1/2 cup cubed, cooked potatoes**

Dash cayenne (optional)

Salt and pepper to taste

Sauté bacon until crisp. Remove from pot and reserve. Sauté onion and pepper in bacon drippings until tender. Add parsley and corn and return bacon to pot. Bring ingredients to a boil; simmer 5 minutes.

Add undiluted soup and stir until blended. Add milk and water and heat until near boiling. Stir in potatoes, blending well. Season to taste. (Add milk, as needed, for desired thickness.)

Yield: 6 servings

SAN DOMINGO CREEK CRAB

Always gets raves as an elegant luncheon entree or appetizer.

2 3-ounce packages cream cheese, softened

1 small onion, finely grated

8 ounces plain yogurt

1 envelope unflavored gelatin, dissolved in 1/4 cup cold water

1 pound crabmeat

1/4 cup mayonnaise

1/2 teaspoon curry powder

1/4 teaspoon prepared horseradish (optional)

Heat cream cheese and onion on low heat until melted, stirring frequently. Add yogurt and dissolved gelatin.

Add crabmeat, mayonnaise, curry powder, and horseradish. Mix well and put into 1-quart mold that has been lightly sprayed with vegetable oil spray.

Refrigerate until stiff, approximately 5 hours (can be made the day before serving). Unmold on bed of lettuce and serve.

Prepare in advance. Yield: 6 to 8 luncheon servings

MOLDED CRANBERRY·
CORNUCOPIA

1 quart fresh cranberries
2 cups sugar
3 tablespoons unflavored gelatin (3 envelopes)
3/4 cup cold water
2 cups boiling water
1 cup nut meats, chopped
1 cup crushed pineapple with juice
1/2 cup celery, sliced thin
1 cup halved grapes

Thanksgiving can't come to a certain house in St. Michaels unless this colorful salad accompanies the turkey.

Coarsely grind or chop cranberries. Place in a large bowl. Add the sugar and gelatin which has been soaked in the cold water. Pour the boiling water over all and stir to dissolve sugar and gelatin.

Let cool and add nut meats, pineapple and juice, celery, and grapes. Pour into a 12- by 7-inch pan and chill.

Cut into squares and serve with salad dressing or whipped cream.

Prepare in advance. Yield: 16 servings

Mystery Salad

See if your guests can detect the mystery ingredients.

3 3-ounce packages raspberry gelatin
1-1/4 cups hot water
3 1-pound cans stewed tomatoes
6 to 8 drops Tabasco sauce

Sour Cream Dressing:
1 pint sour cream
1 tablespoon horseradish
1/4 teaspoon salt
3/4 teaspoon sugar

Dissolve gelatin in hot water. Stir in the stewed tomatoes, breaking up the tomatoes into smaller pieces with a spoon. Add Tabasco sauce. Pour into lightly oiled 3-quart mold. Chill overnight.

Unmold on greens. Mix all dressing ingredients well and fill center of mold with sour cream dressing.

Prepare in advance.   Yield: 12 servings

Under the Sea Salad

Make plenty . . . and hope you are fortunate enough to have left-overs.

2-1/2 cups shell macaroni, cooked and drained
1 pound cooked crab or shrimp
1 cup cooked or raw peas
1 cup chopped celery
1/2 cup chopped red onion
1/4 cup snipped dill *or* 1 tablespoon dried dill weed
Dash each pepper and dry mustard
1/2 cup sliced stuffed green olives

Dressing:
1 cup mayonnaise
2 tablespoons wine vinegar
2 teaspoons lemon juice

Combine dressing ingredients.

Mix together all salad ingredients and combine with dressing. Cover and chill.

Best prepared in advance.   Yield: 6 servings

DESSERTS

MISS FREEDOM'S CHOCOLATE CRAB CAKE COOKIES

Known affectionately as "Miss Freedom," this figurehead on display at the Museum has been the subject of many a photo by visitors. In her search for a truly unique crab cake recipe for this collection, Miss Freedom experienced much frustration in determining which ingredients really make the best crab cake. After much experimentation with just the right ingredients and proportions, she came up with her own very special recipe.

The Chesapeake Bay Maritime Museum is deeply grateful for her generosity in sharing this original, never before published recipe.

1-1/2 cups sifted all purpose flour
1/2 cup baking cocoa
2 teaspoons baking powder
1/2 teaspoon baking soda
1/4 teaspoon salt
1/2 cup butter, softened
1 teaspoon vanilla extract
1 15-ounce can cream of coconut
1/2 cup sugar
2 eggs
1 14-ounce package shredded coconut
1 12-ounce package semi-sweet chocolate morsels

Sift flour with cocoa, baking powder, baking soda, and salt into a medium size mixing bowl; set aside. In a large mixing bowl, cream butter with an electric mixer; add vanilla, cream of coconut, and sugar, beating at high speed for about one minute. Add eggs one at a time, beating well after each addition. On low speed, add dry ingredients, beating just enough to blend. Stir in coconut and chocolate morsels by hand.

Leaving about two inches between each, place rounded table-spoonsful of batter on foil-lined baking sheets; bake at 375 degrees for 15 minutes. (**Note:** If baking more than one pan at a time, rotate the pans top to bottom and front to back halfway through baking.) Crab cakes are done when they spring back if lightly touched in the center; do not overbake.

Yield: 36 to 40 crab cake cookies

CAULK COVE COOKIES

So rich—so good!

1/2 cup butter
1/2 cup brown sugar
1 cup sifted flour
1 cup brown sugar
2 tablespoons flour
1/4 teaspoon baking powder
1/2 teaspoon salt
1 cup chopped pecans
1 cup shredded coconut
2 beaten eggs
1 teaspoon vanilla

FROSTING:
1-1/2 cups powdered sugar
2 tablespoons orange juice
1 tablespoon lemon juice
Grated rind of 1 orange and 1 lemon

In medium bowl, cream 1/2 cup butter. Add 1/2 cup brown sugar and 1 cup sifted flour. Mix well and place in a well-buttered 8-inch by 14-inch pan. Bake 15 minutes at 350 degrees.

In medium bowl, stir together 1 cup brown sugar, 2 tablespoons flour, 1/4 teaspoon baking powder and 1/2 teaspoon salt. Add 1 cup chopped pecans and 1 cup shredded coconut. Mix together.

In small bowl, combine 2 eggs and 1 teaspoon vanilla. Add to dry ingredients. Spread over partially-baked mixture. Return to oven for 30 minutes.

In medium bowl, cream together all frosting ingredients and spread on warm cake. Cut in squares and cool.

Yield: 28 2-inch squares

Sand Tarts

Splurge on these favorite cookies, done up in a no-cholesterol version.

1/4 pound margarine
2/3 cup brown sugar
1 teaspoon vanilla
2 egg whites
1-1/3 cups flour
1/4 teaspoon salt
1/2 teaspoon baking powder
Cinnamon and sugar mixture
Nutmeats or candied cherries

Cream together margarine, sugar and vanilla. Add one egg white and beat.

Sift together flour, salt and baking powder, and add to mixture.

Chill dough several hours. Roll dough into balls the size of a marble and place on an ungreased cookie sheet. Flatten balls with a cloth-covered flat-bottom glass that has been dipped in flour.

Brush top of cookies with one slightly beaten egg white and sprinkle cinnamon and sugar mixture over top. Decorate with broken nutmeats or cherries.

Bake at 325 degrees for 6 to 8 minutes or until brown on edges.

Yield: 50 cookies

PINEAPPLE MINT SQUARES •————————

CRUST
1 cup flour
1/2 cup pecans, chopped
1/4 cup firmly packed brown sugar
1/2 cup butter ♥

FILLING
1 20-ounce can crushed pineapple with juice
1 3-ounce package lime gelatin
1 8-ounce package cream cheese ♥
1 cup sugar
1 cup heavy cream ♥
1/8 teaspoon peppermint extract

GLAZE
1/2 cup semi-sweet chocolate morsels
1/3 cup evaporated milk
1 tablespoon butter ♥
1/4 teaspoon peppermint extract

A touch of mint enlivens both the fruit filling and chocolate glaze in this delicious dessert.

Combine first three ingredients; then cut in butter until fine. Press into bottom of greased 12-×-8 × 2-inch baking dish. Bake at 400 degrees for 12 to 15 minutes. Cool.

Drain pineapple juice into saucepan and bring just to boiling point. Add lime gelatin and stir until dissolved. Allow to cool. Beat cream cheese and sugar together and add to cooled gelatin mixture. Stir in crushed pineapple. Chill until thick but not set.

Whip heavy cream and peppermint extract in small bowl until thick. Fold into pineapple-cheese mixture. Spoon over baked crust. Refrigerate while preparing glaze.

Melt chocolate chips in evaporated milk over low heat, stirring occasionally. Add butter and peppermint extract. Spoon glaze over filling and spread carefully. Chill at least 4 hours.

Prepare in advance.   Yield: 12 servings

Low cholesterol conversion:
For crust, substitute 1/2 cup no-cholesterol mayonnaise for butter. For filling, use imitation rather than regular cream cheese. In place of heavy cream, use 2/3 cup evaporated non-fat skim milk. Chill in a small bowl until ice crystals form before whipping. In glaze, substitute margarine for butter and use non-fat skim evaporated milk.

189

Pecan Squares

1/2 cup shortening

1 cup granulated sugar

2 eggs, well beaten

1 teaspoon vanilla

1-1/2 cups sifted all purpose flour

1 teaspoon salt

1 teaspoon baking powder

2 egg whites

1 cup brown sugar

3/4 cup pecans, chopped finely

Cream shortening; add granulated sugar gradually and mix well.

Beat eggs with vanilla.

Sift together the flour, salt and baking powder. Alternately add beaten eggs and flour mixture to creamed shortening. Mix well. Spread in greased 9- × 13-inch glass baking pan.

Beat egg whites until stiff. Add brown sugar while continuing to beat. Fold in nut meats and spread evenly over cake mixture. Bake at 375 degrees for 25 minutes. Remove from oven. Cool and cut in squares.

Yield: 24 squares

Lemon or Lime Pastry

This pie crust is delicious with any filling, including quiches, pot pies and tarts. The texture is very smooth and easy to roll out. It never fails.

1-1/2 cups all-purpose flour

1/4 teaspoon salt

1/4 teaspoon baking powder

1 tablespoon sugar

1/2 cup shortening

1 beaten egg

1 tablespoon lemon (or lime) juice

1/2 teaspoon grated lemon (or lime) rind

3 tablespoons water

Into large bowl sift flour, salt, baking powder and sugar. Cut in shortening until crumbly. In small bowl combine egg, lemon (or lime) juice and rind, and water. Add 4 tablespoons of the liquid mixture to dry ingredients. Mix lightly with fork at first; then form a ball with hands (do not overwork dough).

Roll out on a floured surface into a circle 1 inch larger than a 10-inch pie pan. Trim edges and roll under around rim. Bake at 425 degrees for 10 minutes.

Yield: One 10-inch pie crust

BLUEBERRY PIE

1 quart fresh blueberries
3/4 cup sugar
3/4 cup water
1 tablespoon flour
Salt
1/4 cup water
1 baked pie shell (*See* Lemon or Lime Pastry)
1/2 cup heavy cream, whipped

This blueberry pie was once deemed the "best in the country" by no less an authority than Duncan Hines. Don't you agree?

Cook 1 cup blueberries, 3/4 cup sugar and 3/4 cup water until berries are soft. Combine 1 tablespoon flour, a pinch of salt, and 1/4 cup water; mix until smooth. Stir flour mixture into cooked berries and cook over medium-low heat, stirring frequently, until thickened.

Fill pie shell with remainder of blueberries. Strain cooked berries over raw berries, discarding that which won't go through the strainer.

Chill in refrigerator for at least 3 hours. Cover with whipped cream and serve.

Prepare in advance.

Yield: 8 servings

COGNAC CHIFFON PIE

An unexpected pleasure, this pie will conclude any dinner in high spirits.

5 egg yolks
3/4 cup sugar
1 envelope unflavored gelatin
1/4 cup water
1/2 cup cognac
1-1/2 cups heavy cream
1 10-inch or deep 9-inch graham cracker crust, baked and cooled
2 tablespoons shaved chocolate

Beat egg yolks until thick and lemon colored. Gradually beat in sugar.

Soften gelatin in water and add 1/4 cup cognac. Heat over boiling water until gelatin dissolves. Pour gelatin mixture into egg yolks, stirring briskly. Stir in remaining cognac.

Whip 1 cup cream until stiff and fold into egg mixture. Pour filling into crust and chill.

Whip 1/2 cup cream and use to decorate chilled pie. Sprinkle shaved chocolate over top.

Prepare in advance.   Yield: One 9- or 10-inch pie

LEMON CREAM PUFFS

You might choose fresh raspberries or blueberries in season to nestle in these cloud-light puffs.

4 tablespoons margarine
1/2 cup boiling water
1/2 cup sifted all-purpose flour
1/4 teaspoon salt
2 eggs

LEMON CREAM FILLING
6 tablespoons butter or margarine
3/4 cup sugar
4 large egg yolks
5 tablespoons fresh lemon juice
1 cup heavy cream
16 fresh strawberries, washed and hulled
Powdered sugar

Place margarine in 1-quart saucepan with 1/2 cup boiling water. Cook over high heat until margarine melts. Turn down heat and add flour and salt. Stir vigorously until it leaves the side of pan. (Be sure when placing spoon that no margarine oozes out.)

Remove pan from heat and add 1 egg. Beat until smooth. Add second egg and beat again until you have a smooth, shiny dough. Drop by tablespoons onto ungreased cookie sheet. Bake at 400 degrees for 10 minutes, then reduce to 350 degrees and bake for 25 minutes. Cool on a rack.

In medium saucepan, melt butter or margarine over medium-low heat. Stir in sugar and cook, stirring, for 1 or 2 minutes. Remove from heat and whisk in egg yolks and lemon juice. Return to medium-low heat and cook, stirring constantly, until mixture thickens, about 5 minutes. Remove from heat and cool to room temperature.

Beat heavy cream until stiff and fold into cooled lemon mixture. Cover and chill. When ready to serve, slice tops off puff shells and spoon about 2 tablespoons of lemon cream mixture into each shell. Set a strawberry on the cream and replace top of puff shell. Dust with powdered sugar.

Shells may be made a day ahead.

Fill just before serving.   Yield: 16 cream puffs

BLUEBERRY SLUMP •———————————————————

3 cups fresh blueberries (frozen, in off-season)
3/4 cup sugar
1/2 cup water
1/4 teaspoon cinnamon
6 slices bread, crusts removed, buttered
Sweetened whipped cream

Combine blueberries, sugar, water, and cinnamon in saucepan. Bring to a boil; simmer for 10 minutes.

Lay two slices buttered bread in 8- × 4-inch loaf pan. (Cut bread if necessary to fit the pan.) Pour 1/3 of blueberry mixture over bread. Repeat this twice more.

Refrigerate the Slump for 2 to 3 hours or more. Serve with sweetened whipped cream.

Prepare in advance.   Yield: 4 to 6 servings

Cultivated blueberries are fine, of course, but for the very best taste use wild blueberries, preferably ones that you picked on your walk today.

LIME CHEESECAKE

The tang of lime juice and easy no-bake preparation make this cheesecake truly unique.

CRUST:

1/3 cup butter or margarine, melted

1/4 cup sugar

1 cup graham cracker crumbs

1 cup shredded coconut

1/2 cup sliced almonds

FILLING:

1 envelope unflavored gelatin

1/2 cup sugar

4 egg yolks, beaten with 2 tablespoons water

1 tablespoon grated lime peel

1/2 cup fresh lime juice

2 8-ounce packages cream cheese, softened

4 egg whites

1/4 cup sugar

1 cup heavy cream

Whipped cream and lime slices for garnish

Combine crust ingredients and press onto bottom of 9-inch springform pan. Chill while preparing filling.

In a medium saucepan, combine gelatin, 1/2 cup sugar, egg-and-water mixture. Cook over low heat, stirring constantly, until gelatin is dissolved, about 5 minutes. Remove from heat; stir in lime peel and juice. Cool to room temperature.

In a large bowl, beat softened cream cheese until fluffy. Blend cooled lime mixture into cream cheese.

In a medium bowl, beat egg whites until soft peaks form. Add 1/4 cup sugar, a tablespoon at a time, and beat until stiff peaks form. Fold egg whites into cream cheese-lime mixture.

Beat whipping cream until stiff. Fold into cream cheese-lime mixture. Pour over prepared crust; cover and chill overnight. Garnish with whipped cream and lime slices, if desired.

Prepare in advance. Yield: 10 to 12 servings

TIPPLER'S TORTE

3 cups pecans

6 eggs, separated

1-1/2 cups sugar

3 tablespoons flour

1 teaspoon salt

3 tablespoons rum

1 cup heavy cream

4 tablespoons powdered sugar

1 6-ounce package semi-sweet chocolate pieces

1/2 cup sour cream

Yo ho ho . . . there's a measure of rum in both cake and filling of this scrumptious dessert.

Put pecans in the blender (1 cup at a time) and whirl until very finely chopped.

Beat egg yolks until very light, then beat in sugar, flour, salt, 2 tablespoons of rum, and nuts. Mix well; then fold in egg whites that have been beaten until stiff but not dry.

Pour into 3 8-inch or 2 10-inch layer cake pans that have been lined with waxed paper and buttered. Bake in a pre-heated oven at 350 degrees until gentle finger pressure fails to leave a mark, about 25 minutes. Cool and remove from pans.

A few hours before serving, put cake layers together with a filling of the cream whipped with the powdered sugar and 1 tablespoon of rum. For icing, melt the chocolate bits; fold in the sour cream and spread over the top of the cake.

Prepare in advance.   Yield: One large cake

GRAPENUT-LEMON PUFF

This dessert bakes itself into three layers—crust, custard, and sauce. A dollop of whipped cream on top makes four.

1/2 cup butter

2 cups sugar

4 egg yolks, well beaten

4 tablespoons flour

6 tablespoons grapenuts

2 cups milk

Grated rind and juice of 2 lemons

4 egg whites, beaten stiff

Sugar

Cream butter and 2 cups sugar thoroughly. Blend in egg yolks until smooth. Blend in flour, then fold in grapenuts. Stir in milk, lemon juice and rind.

Gently fold in egg whites, well mixed but not over-stirred. Pour into buttered 9- × 9-inch baking dish and sprinkle with sugar. Place in a pan of water and bake at 375 degrees for 50 to 60 minutes.

Yield: 6 servings

FRIENDSHIP HALL CHOCOLATE DECADENT CAKE

Here's an A+ offering from the famous Eastern Shore cooking school.

1 pound dark sweet chocolate

1 stick plus 2 tablespoons unsalted butter

4 extra large eggs

1-1/2 tablespoons granulated sugar

1-1/2 tablespoons cake flour

1/8 teaspoon cream of tartar

1 cup whipping cream

1 tablespoon powdered sugar

1 teaspoon vanilla

Preheat oven to 400 degrees. Cut parchment paper for an 8-inch round cake pan.

Slowly melt chocolate and butter in top of double boiler (do not let bottom touch water). Pour into a large mixing bowl.

Combine eggs and sugar in another large mixing bowl and whip at high speed until mixture has tripled in size. Slowly add cake flour mixed with cream of tartar.

Pour about one-third of egg mixture into chocolate-butter mixture and beat to lighten. Gently fold in remaining egg mixture and pour into baking pan.

Bake for 10 minutes. Lightly place a piece of foil over cake and bake another 4 minutes. Remove pan from oven and place on rack to cool. When cool, cover with foil. Place in freezer and freeze several hours.

About 30 minutes to an hour before serving, remove from freezer. Remove foil and swirl about 1 minute in pan of hot water. Run knife around edge. Invert cake on serving plate and peel off parchment paper. Pipe or spread on cream whipped with powdered sugar and vanilla.

Prepare in advance. ·Yield: 10-12 servings

PECAN CAKE

5 eggs
1 box light brown sugar
1 cup white sugar
1 cup vegetable shortening
1 stick butter or margarine
3 cups flour
1 cup milk
1-1/2 cups broken pecans
1/2 teaspoon baking powder
1/2 teaspoon salt
1 teaspoon vanilla

This recipe has been handed down in one family for three generations. Delicious anytime, but a "must" for Christmas.

Combine all ingredients in large bowl of electric mixer and beat on medium speed until well blended.

Line bottom of tube pan with waxed paper and pour in batter. Bake at 350 degrees for 1 to 1-1/4 hours until done.

Yield: 12 to 16 servings

HOT MILK CAKE

*Hold on to your will power—
it's difficult to stop after just
one slice.*

4 eggs

1-3/4 cups sugar

2 cups sifted flour

2 teaspoons baking powder

1/4 pound butter heated in 1 cup milk

1 teaspoon vanilla

1 teaspoon cinnamon

1 tablespoon sugar

Beat eggs well. Beat sugar into eggs, then add flour and baking powder and continue beating. Add butter heated in milk; stir in vanilla.

Pour into greased and floured tube pan. Bake at 375 degrees for 45 minutes. Cool on rack for 15 minutes and turn out of pan.

While cake is warm, sprinkle with cinnamon and sugar.

Yield: 10 to 12 servings

CREAMY PUMPKIN PUDDING

*Enjoy a Halloween "treat" at
jack-o-lantern time by
preparing this pudding with
fresh, cooked pumpkin.*

1 cup fresh, mashed, cooked pumpkin (canned may be substituted)

1 tablespoon maple syrup or pancake syrup

1/2 teaspoon ground cinnamon

1/4 teaspoon ground cloves

1/4 teaspoon salt

1-1/2 cups milk

1 3-1/4-ounce package vanilla instant pudding mix

1/2 cup heavy cream, whipped

Combine pumpkin, syrup, cinnamon, cloves and salt. Gradually blend in milk and pudding mix. Beat slowly with electric mixer until thick, about 1 minute.

Fold in whipped cream and spoon into dessert dishes. Chill 1 hour.

Yield: 6 servings

Steamed Cranberry Pudding with Vanilla Cream Sauce

PUDDING:
1-1/2 cups flour
1 teaspoon baking powder
1-1/2 cups cranberries
1/2 cup dark molasses
2 teaspoons baking soda
Hot water
1/2 cup raisins (optional)
1/2 cup chopped pecans (optional)

SAUCE:
1/2 cup butter
1 cup sugar
1/2 cup heavy cream
1 teaspoon vanilla *or* rum

This recipe is easily doubled. Not only will you be able to use up all the cranberries in the package at once, but you will also have a pudding to put away in the freezer.

Sift flour and baking powder together into a mixing bowl. Add washed cranberries and stir gently so flour coats the berries.

Put the 1/2 cup molasses into a 1-cup measure and add baking soda. Fill the 1-cup measure to overflowing with *hot* water, stirring to activate the soda. Dump quickly into berry mix and stir well. Add raisins and nuts. Pour into 1-pound coffee can or favorite mold.

To steam, put water into bottom of kettle, roaster or pan to accommodate mold. Put a wire or wooden rack in bottom of pan. The water should come to the top of the rack but not cover it. Cover pan and bring water to a boil.

When steam rises, put mold onto rack. Do not cover the mold, but do cover the pan. Steam over low heat for 2 hours. Keep some hot water close by in case you need to add more. Peek in occasionally—don't let the pan go dry.

Sauce: Over low heat melt the butter and sugar. Add cream and heat through, but do not let it boil. Stir in vanilla or rum. Spoon sweet sauce over servings of tangy steamed pudding.

Note: If you are using a pudding that you have frozen, defrost, wrap it in foil, and tuck it in the oven to warm while you are having dinner.

Yield: 4 to 6 servings

PERSIMMON PUDDING

Scout out the nearest persimmon tree and treat yourself to this tangy dessert.

2-1/4 cups flour
1/2 cup sugar
1 cup packed dark brown sugar
1/2 tablespoon baking powder
1 teaspoon baking soda
1 teaspoon cinnamon
1 teaspoon allspice
1/2 teaspoon salt
2 cups persimmon pulp
1 cup buttermilk
2 eggs
Whipped cream for garnish

Combine all ingredients except whipped cream in large bowl. Mix at low speed just until batter is smooth.

Spread batter in two greased 9- × 9-inch baking pans; level batter with spatula. Bake at 350 degrees for 60 minutes or until a toothpick inserted in the center comes out clean.

Serve warm or cooled, garnished with whipped cream.

Prepare in advance.   Yield: 18 servings

Fuzzy Navel Freeze

3/4 cup fresh orange juice
1/4 cup peach schnapps
1 cup sugar
6 egg yolks
1 pint heavy cream
1 teaspoon grated orange peel
9 medium-size Navel oranges (*or* 2 fresh peaches)
Fresh mint leaves

The popular morning drink lends its refreshing blend of orange and peach flavors to this beautifully presented dessert.

Combine orange juice, peach schnapps and sugar in a medium saucepan and cook to 235 degrees (soft ball stage) on a candy thermometer.

Place egg yolks in top of double boiler over hot water. With a portable mixer, slowly beat hot orange syrup into egg yolks. Continue beating until thick and light colored, 5 to 7 minutes. Place top of double boiler in cold water and continue beating until mixture cools. Remove from cold water.

Whip cream until stiff and fold into orange mixture. Fold in orange peel.

Slice tops off 8 Navel oranges. Hold over bowl to catch fruit and juice, and remove fruit with a grapefruit knife. (Reserve orange pulp and juice for another use.) Turn oranges upside-down on paper towels to drain briefly.

Fill each orange shell with 1/8 of Fuzzy Navel mixture, mounding on top. Cover and freeze several hours or overnight. To serve, thinly slice remaining orange. Slit each slice from inner edge of peel across to opposite side, then twist halves away from each other and place on mounded mixture. Add a mint leaf or two to complete garnish.

Alternate presentation: Smooth Fuzzy Navel mixture into 1-1/2-quart serving bowl and freeze several hours or overnight. Just before serving, peel and slice peaches and arrange pinwheel-fashion on top of mixture. Garnish with mint leaves.

Prepare in advance.   Yield: 8 servings

HERE'S TO YOUR HEALTH

Seeking a healthful diet? We are pleased to include several recipes showing low-cholesterol or no-cholesterol alternatives. The ingredient substitutions and changes in preparation technique required to convert the recipe to a low-cholesterol recipe are designated by the ♥ symbol. It should be noted, however, that while these recipes may contain little or no cholesterol, the recipes are not necessarily low-fat alternatives. Therefore, additional care may need to be taken in meal preparation for those with further diet restrictions.

To facilitate healthful cooking, we include the following suggestions for substitutions to low-cholesterol ingredients and for low-cholesterol food preparation techniques.

INGREDIENT SUBSTITUTION CHART

Instead of . . .	Use . . .
Bacon	Imitation bacon bits
Butter or solid shortening	Vegetable cooking spray; liquid vegetable oil, especially canola oil or olive oil; margarine made from liquid vegetable oil (not partially-hydrogenated vegetable oil)
Cheese	Cholesterol-free and lactose-free cheese substitutes for cheddar, mozzarella and cream cheeses (commercially available)
Chocolate	Cocoa powder
Cream or whole milk	Skim milk or evaporated skim milk
Mayonnaise	Cholesterol-free mayonnaise (commercially available)
Salt	Pepper and dried or fresh herbs
Shrimp and lobster	Sea Legs (commercially-available frozen prepared whitefish), scallops or crabmeat
Sour Cream	Non-fat yogurt; low-fat yogurt blended with buttermilk until smooth; or no-cholesterol sour cream substitute (commercially available)
Whole eggs	Egg whites (2 instead of a whole egg); low-cholesterol egg substitute (frozen)

LOW-CHOLESTEROL FOOD PREPARATION TECHNIQUES

Instead of . . .	Use . . .
Buttered bread crumb topping	Plain bread crumbs placed on top of food then sprayed with vegetable cooking spray; reduce time under broiler for browning.
Chicken broth (with fat)	Place chicken broth in refrigerator overnight before day of food preparation; skim off hardened fat which rises to top before using.
Meat/poultry (with fat)	Purchase lean cuts, remove all skin and visible fat before cooking; light meat of poultry is leaner than dark meat.
Roux/thickening with flour	Arrowroot (preferred), cornstarch, potato starch; arrowroot and cornstarch should be dissolved in water before use; then avoid boiling after adding into cooking.
Whipped cream	Whip skim milk with nonfat milk powder or use evaporated skim milk; add softened gelatin before whipping to stabilize.

RECIPE INDEX

Recipe Contributors

Betty Adams
Mark Adams
Deborah Barrows
Helen Bennett
Jean Berger
Peter Black
Elizabeth Bosse
Heidi Brace
Mickey Breen
Benita Brown
Mary Bullen
Julienne Burns
Eleanor Kennedy Buschman
Zetta Carver
Dennis Cassidy
Spry Cheezum
Joan Cole
Joan H. Comer
Jean Cooper
Beckie and Paul Curtis
Jane Davis
Linda Davis
Mrs. George W. DeFranceaux
Barrie Dettling
Mary Doeller
Jack Doetzer
Laura Jankowski Dowling
Mrs. F. S. Dudley
Marjorie R. Eby
Elizabeth Edgcomb
Mrs. Charles L. Fairbank, Jr.
Judy Fankhanel
Frances W. Ferguson
Mary Fiedler
Betsy Fisk
Nancy Fletcher
Mrs. Samuel Lyles Freeland
Gloria Frost
Nancy German
Louise A. Giese
Ginny Graebert
Barbara Gschwind
Betts Guthrie
Gaby Haab

Alice Haddaway
Bill Harper
Mrs. Roderick Lyons Hickey, Sr.
Mrs. Roderick Lyons Hickey, Jr.
Mary and Van Holston
Bé Holt
Jack Holt
Jim Holt
Marianna M. Hornor
Tom Howell
Mary Louise Humiston
Lynne A. Jarrell
Mr. and Mrs. Paul Johnstone
Martha Jones
Mrs. C. L. Juppe
Peg Keller
Mildred Kemp
Alverta Kilbourn
Mrs. A. C. Kramer
Doris Lubbers
Sheila Mann
Bobbie and Junie Marshall
Nathalie Dodson May
Lori Mazza
Rose Mary Mazza
Harriett McConnell
Kate McCormick
Barton McGuire
Mrs. Eugene Meyung
Marcia Myers
Don Ney
Ida Olcese
Mary Ellen Olcese
Bob Olwine
Tarz Palomba
Frances Parker
Dody Welsh Parris
Ed Payne
R. Henny Perkinson
Ellen Plummer
Marilyn Pugh
Tamara L. Pusey
Ann Rybon
Martha Schuette

Mary Ann Schwanda
Richard and John Scofield
Emily Shane
Mildred Shores
Ann Simmons
Martha Singer
Ginny Slocum
Bob Smith
Jean Snyder
Samuel S. Spaulding
Steve Spurry
Lillian Thomas
Ron Thomas
Dr. M. Fred Tidwell
Deenie Tyler
Erle Ukkleberg
John R. Valliant
Lise A. Valliant
Ann Watson
David Webber
Betty Wehse
Ruth Weller
Valerie Youngs
Barbara S. Zimmer

PICTURE CREDITS

FROM A LIGHTHOUSE WINDOW
Recipes and Recollections from the Chesapeake Bay Maritime Museum

Please Print:

Name: _____

Address _____

City/State/Zip: _____

Telephone: ( ) _____

Charge to: VISA _____ MasterCard _____

Account No. _____

Exp. Date _____

Signature _____

☐ **Check enclosed (Make checks payable to CBMM Cookbook)**

Museum Member _____ Yes _____No *Please Send Information on How to Become a Museum Member* _____

If Museum Member, Complete This Section (Price $17.95)

Please send me _____copies of
From A Lighthouse Window
at $17.95 each $_____

Maryland residents add 5% sales tax
($.90 each book)   _____

Postage: add $5.00 for the first book,
plus $1.50 for each additional book.   _____

If Non-Member, Complete This Section (Price $19.95)

Please send me _____copies of
From A Lighthouse Window
at $19.95 each $_____

Maryland residents add 5% sales tax
($1.00 each book)   _____

Postage: add $5.00 for the first book,
plus $1.50 for each additional book   _____

TOTAL $_____

Mail this form to:

FROM A LIGHTHOUSE WINDOW
CHESAPEAKE BAY MARITIME MUSEUM
Mill St., P.O. Box 636
St. Michaels, MD 21663-0636

· ·

FROM A LIGHTHOUSE WINDOW
Recipes and Recollections from the Chesapeake Bay Maritime Museum

Please Print:

Name: _____

Address _____

City/State/Zip: _____

Telephone: ( ) _____

Charge to: VISA _____ MasterCard _____

Account No. _____

Exp. Date _____

Signature _____

☐ **Check enclosed (Make checks payable to CBMM Cookbook)**

Museum Member _____ Yes _____No *Please Send Information on How to Become a Museum Member* _____

If Museum Member, Complete This Section (Price $17.95)

Please send me _____copies of
From A Lighthouse Window
at $17.95 each $_____

Maryland residents add 5% sales tax
($.90 each book)   _____

Postage: add $5.00 for the first book,
plus $1.50 for each additional book.   _____

If Non-Member, Complete This Section (Price $19.95)

Please send me _____copies of
From A Lighthouse Window
at $19.95 each $_____

Maryland residents add 5% sales tax
($1.00 each book)   _____

Postage: add $5.00 for the first book,
plus $1.50 for each additional book.   _____

TOTAL $_____

Mail this form to:

FROM A LIGHTHOUSE WINDOW
CHESAPEAKE BAY MARITIME MUSEUM
Mill St., P.O. Box 636
St. Michaels, MD 21663-0636

FROM A LIGHTHOUSE WINDOW
CHESAPEAKE BAY MARITIME MUSEUM
Mill St., P.O. Box 636
St. Michaels, MD 21663-0636

. . . .

FROM A LIGHTHOUSE WINDOW
CHESAPEAKE BAY MARITIME MUSEUM
Mill St., P.O. Box 636
St. Michaels, MD 21663-0636